Pebble Polishing

A guide to collecting, tumble polishing and making baroque jewellery

Pebble Polishing

A guide to collecting, tumble polishing and making baroque jewellery

by

Edward Fletcher

London

Blandford Press

First published 1972
© 1972 Blandford Press Ltd,
167 High Holborn, London WC1V 6PH

ISBN 0 7137 0566 3

Text set in 11 on 13 Bembo and
printed in Great Britain by
Unwin Brothers Limited
Woking and London

List of Contents

Acknowledgements

The author and publishers are grateful to the following who have helped to produce this book:

Michael Allman, F.I.I.P., F.R.P.S., who took the colour and most of the black-and-white photographs for the book;

John Wood, who drew the illustrations;

Gemrocks Ltd, Holborn, London E.C.1, stockists of tumble-polishing machines and foreign stones illustrated, who devoted a great deal of time and care to checking the manuscript and setting up many of the black-and-white photographs;

M. L. Beach (Products) Ltd, Church Street, Twickenham, manufacturers of tumble-polishing and other lapidary machines, who supplied Figs. 42(a), 43, 44 and 45.

Roland Phelps, then employed at Gemrocks Ltd, who supplied the pebbles for Plates 1, 2 and 3 and the fossil for Fig. 11;

British Travel Authority for Figs. 1, 2, 4 and the endpapers;

Institute of Geological Sciences (Crown Copyright) for Fig. 8.

Pebble-collecting, which was well known in our grand-parents' day as a casual pastime for those infrequent one-day visits to the seaside, has come back into fashion lately in a big way. At the same time it has developed into a creative, absorbing occupation for the hobbyist, offering tremendous personal pleasure and satisfaction.

Mass production of cheap costume jewellery has enjoyed a boom in recent years. Millions of pounds are spent annually on rings, bracelets, pendants, baubles and beads manufactured from coloured glass and plastics and sold in chain stores up and down the country. The discerning woman, anxious to acquire something different, something unique in costume jewellery, finds little to satisfy her tastes in a market where 90 per cent of the goods are of a very low standard.

It is to fill this gap that thousands of women (and not a few men) have seized on pebble-collecting and tumble-polishing as a means of making their own unique and beautiful jewellery. Unlike their grandmothers, who relied on skilled lapidaries to transform their finds to gems, todays' collectors can polish and mount their pebbles easily, quickly and at little expense. This has been made possible thanks to the recent introduction of tumble-polishing machines, epoxy resin and inexpensive jewellery fittings, all of which are extremely simple to use. To work efficiently, a tumble-polisher requires nothing more than connection to the household electricity supply, some pebbles, a suitable abrasive grit or polish and ordinary tap water. It will transform humble beach pebbles into highly polished gems with the minimum of care and attention. Epoxy resin is simply strong, permanent glue and modern jewellery fittings come in a wide variety of shapes and sizes, catering for every taste. With a little patience and artistic flair anyone can make jewellery of the highest quality.

Of course, the other great attraction of the hobby is that it combines out-door fun with indoor pleasure. Collecting the pebbles is as exciting as making the jewellery. Britain's beaches abound with beautiful stones; amethysts, cornelians, jaspers, agates, milky quartz and serpentine can all be found quite readily at a hundred and one different holiday locations. Whole summers can be spent in happy and successful hunting—perhaps on a Cornish beach seeking pairs of matched serpentine pebbles for earrings; at Whitby searching the beach for jet; in Suffolk where cornelians and amber (known to the ancients as the tears of the Sun God, Apollo) can be found; or more likely simply collecting some of the countless millions of more humble yet just as colourful pebbles which attract the eye on almost every beach in Britain.

Detailed knowledge of geology is not essential to make pebble-collecting and polishing worthwhile. Knowing a few simple rules—and what *not* to collect—is all that is required. Collecting the pebbles will almost certainly stimulate a desire for a greater knowledge and it will not be long before a newcomer to the hobby begins to recognize most of his finds. With this knowledge will come deep appreciation of this truly fascinating subject and its possibilities.

The purpose of this book is to take the beginner step by step through every stage in baroque jewellery-making: where to find the pebbles, which ones to collect, buying a tumbler, achieving first-class results when polishing, and how to mount the polished stones on the fittings. For those who do find that they want to study the subject in more depth, I have included a brief chapter on foreign stones and one on more advanced equipment. The time will come when you will want to polish some of the exotic stones which are now imported into Britain from all over the world, for example Tiger's eye, Malachite, Rose quartz or Snowflake obsidian; or try your hand at grinding, cutting or even faceting stones. Finally, there is a list of the main lapidary suppliers situated throughout the country, where the latest machines and equipment are available.

No matter where you live in Britain you can drive to a shingle beach in a couple of hours, and as every stretch of shingle will present you with a million pebbles it might seem a little superfluous to begin this book by telling you where to go. Almost anywhere is good, but there are certain coasts which can rightly claim to be better than others. My aim here is to give you a gentle push in the direction of those better beaches.

Most of us like variety and that is just what the best beaches have—a wide variety of colourful and beautiful semi-precious pebbles which are yours for the taking. Luckily these special areas are very fairly distributed—four in England and Wales and three in Scotland—and while any reader lucky enough to live in one of these seven areas is to be envied, the rest of us can hardly grumble. Nature has shared her prizes so well that anyone should be able to reach at least one really outstanding area and return home with all the pebbles he or she can carry within a day. Even more fortunately, these seven extra-special areas happen to be on coasts with popular seaside resorts.

1 Where to find the pebbles

Fig. 1 The fishing fleet and pebble beach at Hastings, Sussex

You can, if you wish, take a pebble-hunting holiday without forfeiting good hotels, food or entertainment.

The seven best pebble areas are:

The best areas

1 *The West coast of Cornwall*, recommended to readers living west of the Isle of Wight.
2 *The Anglesey area of North Wales*, recommended to readers living in the Birmingham–Liverpool areas.
3 *The Ayrshire coast*, recommended to readers living around Glasgow.
4 *The coasts of Northern Scotland*, recommended to all holiday-makers in Scotland.
5 *The Fifeshire coast*, recommended to readers living in Eastern Scotland.
6 *The East Yorkshire Coast*, recommended to all North of England readers.
7 *The Norfolk and Suffolk coasts*, recommended to readers living in Eastern and South-Eastern England.

Do not let this list of seven best sites deter you in any way from your own local beach or particular beauty spot on the coast. Good pebbles are to be found anywhere. Even the semi-precious pebbles which make the above areas worth visiting *can* be found on other beaches. The pheno-

Fig. 2 Red Wharf Bay, Anglesey

menon known as longshore drift is forever at work in your favour, feeding other beaches with a never-ending supply of new and interesting pebbles.

If you have ever thrown a handful of currants into a basin of flour and stirred vigorously you will understand long-shore drift. The currants are swept along in the direction of your spoon until they are evenly distributed throughout your pudding mixture. On the coast a similar movement goes on. From the tip of Cornwall pebbles are swept eastward along the coast towards the Isle of Wight; from North Wales pebbles move up the coast towards Cumberland; Ayrshire pebbles also travel northward, but once we round the far north of Scotland the direction of drift is southward. Down the coast comes all that is best in Scottish pebbles. Those from Aberdeenshire can be found on the Yorkshire coast, and the wonderful semi-precious pebbles to be found in Yorkshire are in their turn swept southward to join those of Norfolk and Suffolk.

Thus a never-ending movement goes on, providing an inexhaustible supply of pebbles for every stretch of shingle around Britain's 7,000 miles of coastline. The sea is always at work, moving and depositing the shingle which, on most beaches, rests on a shelf of permanent rock. If this rock is on an exposed part of the coast, particularly a long, straight coast, the rate of movement is quite consider-able. Whole beds of shingle can vanish in a single violent storm in such places; while shingle beds on beaches protected by headlands and coves are moved rather less. But whatever your favourite collecting spot, it is certain that the pebbles you cast your eyes over on one visit are not the ones you will pick up and choose from next time.

There cannot be many hobbies which require so little outlay on equipment as pebble-collecting. True, you need a tumble-polishing machine if you are going to polish your finds when you get them home, but the basic raw materials —pebbles—are yours for the taking. You can get

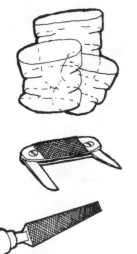

Fig. 3 Basic equipment

by with a pocket handkerchief or a brown paper bag if you find yourself with half an hour to spare on an unexpected visit to the coast. However, several basic items—all of which are certain to be lying around at home—are well worth taking on any expedition. They are:

> three small plastic bags (the ones you buy potatoes in are ideal) to put your pebbles in
> a penknife with a strong blade
> a small steel file.

For most people collecting pebbles is a family activity, with Dad, Mum, the children and even the family dog joining in, so three bags are not so unmanageable as they sound. In the next chapter I will explain how you can group your pebbles in a way which will help you achieve the best results when you go on to polishing. As this grouping can be done during collecting with the aid of your penknife and file, and as you will be placing your pebbles into one of three groups, you can complete the job on the beach by putting each pebble into one of your three bags.

Fig. 4 Cadgwith, Cornwall

Or if you go on your own, you can make do with one large bag and carry out the grouping at home.

The best part of the beach to search for pebbles of a suitable size for your tumbler is down by the water's edge, so it is wise to wear an old pair of sandals or plimsoles. And do not forget to take a warm sweater or jumper, even in summertime. You might spend a couple of hours combing the shingle for the pebbles you need and sea breezes can be quite cold no matter how blue the sky.

Safety

There is nothing dangerous about pebble-collecting. The only possible risk arises from the fact that looking for pebbles is such an absorbing pastime that you might forget that tides come in as often as they go out. On some coasts the tide can sweep in with treacherous speed, so do keep an eye on the sea—especially on any beach backed by cliffs. If there is no way out of an interesting cove up the cliffside, make certain that you give yourself ample time to walk to safety before the tide comes in. The local coastguard is only a telephone call away and can give you reliable information about how long you can safely spend on such beaches.

Remember, too, that steep cliffs can hold other dangers. Confine your searching to the shingle on the beach, well away from the cliff face where rock falls could lead to disaster.

2 Selecting your pebbles

Happily, it is quite unnecessary to possess a detailed knowledge of geology to collect pebbles that will polish well and make up into beautiful jewellery. Nevertheless, the question on every beginner's lips is, 'How do I know which pebbles to collect?' The practical answer is to learn half a dozen basic rules which will help you to eliminate pebbles quite useless for tumble-polishing and to collect suitable ones which attract or please your eye. You *will* make mistakes and your first attempts at polishing are unlikely to be first-class. But you will learn far more by this trial and error method than any reference book could ever teach you.

To the perfectionist this may sound like side-stepping the question. For those who would like to go further into it, I recommend a course in geology and gemology and the books in the bibliography. In a couple of years you will have learnt a great deal about the subject and no doubt have your own views on tumbling. Meanwhile, readers who follow my simpler method of identification will find that their final results are just as good as the results of those who decide to study the subject scientifically.

The basic rules

Size. Always collect small pebbles. Larger ones make excellent door-stops, paperweights and ballast but they do not tumble. Look for pebbles between the size of your smallest fingernail and the top joint of your thumb. One or two slightly larger ones may be included if they are particularly worth having, but bear in mind that your ultimate aim is to make jewellery. You require pebbles suitably sized for earrings, bracelets, necklaces and rings.

Do not make the mistake of collecting pebbles of uniform size. Aim at a good selection between the smallest and largest. Tumblers work more efficiently when loaded with pebbles of different sizes and you will need different sizes when making up your jewellery.

Shape. Beginners usually make the mistake of collecting either all near-perfectly round pebbles or only those which look like the work of an adventurous modern sculptor.

A happy compromise is what you should aim at. Collect a variety of shapes, but consider their usability as you do so. Weird and wonderful shapes have only a limited use in jewellery-making; whereas ovoids, flat discs, spheres and other uniform shapes are all worth collecting.

Amount. The temptation to collect too many pebbles is often hard to resist—especially when you are on a stretch of shingle with an abundant supply of colourful material—but you must learn to discipline yourself. Bear in mind the capacity of your tumbler barrels, the number of jewellery fittings you plan to buy, the length of time until your next visit to the coast and the problems of storage at home.

The removal of large quantities of shingle from beaches is frowned upon by local authorities. Shingle forms a natural barrier against erosion by wave action and its removal is strictly controlled. No one will prevent you from taking away a few pounds of pretty pebbles, but if every visitor to Brighton went home with a couple of hundredweights there would be a big hole in the ground!

What to leave behind. There are far more pebbles on an average beach that will polish than there are pebbles that will not. If you can recognize the ones that will not, you will automatically know the ones that will. Pebbles that will not polish well can all be recognized by their surface appearance and their feel to your fingers. These are the *porous*, the *granular*, the *flaky* and the *veined;* all of them are very soft. Very soft pebbles will not polish in a tumbler. The abrasive power of the grits used in the process is too great; they disintegrate and upset the grinding and polishing sequence in the barrel. (See p. 22.)

(a) *The porous.* These can be quickly spotted. They are the pebbles which stay wet too long. You will often find them well above the waterline and still moist when other pebbles nearby are quite dry. The worst ones will crumble under your fingernail; others will feel very coarse to your touch. They are usually sandstone and probably brown or yellow.

(b) *The granular.* These also stay wet too long, and are

15

Fig. 5(a) Coarse-grained sandstone

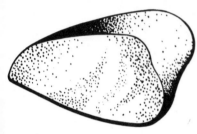

Fig. 5(b) Fine-grained sandstone

Fig. 5(c) Schist

Fig. 5(d) Quartz veins in slate

usually sandstone. They *can* be finely textured but you will probably be able to see the minute grains of sand from which they are formed. They are often collected by beginners because they can be colourful—greens, reds, yellows and browns—but this is simply mineral oxide staining.

(c) *The flaky.* The parallel layers of material which make up these pebbles are usually readily visible to the naked eye. In certain varieties, known as *slates*, each layer represents a single stage in a long process of formation—the laying down and compressing of clay over millions of years. These layers can be flaked off with the point of a knife.

Others, known as *mudstone*, have even closer parallel layers which have been formed from fine mud and these layers can be difficult to see. A knife blade will scratch such pebbles easily. A third and very large group, the *schists*, have the same characteristic layers but often tempt collectors because they contain other mineral particles which impart pretty colours or attractive sparkle.

(d) *The veined.* These cause much trouble to old hands at the game as well as to beginners. They can be extremely beautiful and the temptation to drop one or two into one of your collecting bags is great. Pale pink, deep red, yellow, white and translucent are the colours found, usually as a swirling tracery of veins in finely textured sandstone pebbles. Examine one closely and you will see that the veins stand proud of the general surface. This is because they are composed of much harder material—quartz, feldspar, or jasper—and have resisted erosion far better than the sandstone in the main body of the pebble.

There is another very common type of pebble which you should not collect. This is the badly pitted or cracked specimen of *any* variety. A pebble with a deeply pitted surface will take a long time to grind smooth in your tumbler. Other pebbles will be ready for the next stage in the process long before a pitted one has been worn to smoothness and you will almost certainly have to reject it at some stage. A rare or particularly beautiful pebble which has surface blemishes *can* be saved at the expense of size. This

16

is done either by hand-polishing (a long and slow process) or by putting it through a very prolonged first tumbling phase. The pebble is extracted from the load after a barrel is emptied at the end of the first stage and returned to stock to await the next batch of pebbles going into the barrel for the first time. By doing this three or four times it is possible to wear down the pebble to a point where all surface pitting is removed. It will, however, be greatly reduced in size—a point worth bearing in mind if you are planning to make a piece of jewellery requiring a large pebble. Any badly cracked pebble is likely to fracture during the rugged first stage of tumbling and its sharp edges will not wear down quickly enough to be ready for second-stage grinding at the end of the first run.

The last item on the 'leave-it-behind' list is man-made material. There is a surprising amount on most beaches and you should learn to recognize it. Five man-made materials can be confused with pebbles: brick, concrete, earthenware, china and glass. The ceaseless pounding of the waves and the grinding action of sand can wear fragments of these materials to pebble-shape in a very short time. Corners are knocked off, surfaces smoothed, colours bleached, and a deceptive coating given to the finished shape. Even geologists can be confused. But do not despair: the seeker after pebbles for tumble-polishing is unlikely to be bothered by four of these intruders.

A pebble of brick will be either red or yellow, and when you have examined it closely you will recognize it as brick or else take it for jasper (see pp. 23 & 25) or sandstone. Scratch it with a knife. If it scrapes easily, it is not jasper. You already know that sandstone is unsuitable for polishing and should be rejected. Thus brick pebbles should present no problem. Pebbles of concrete should also be thrown away.

Earthenware and china are also likely to be taken for sandstone, in which case the above test applies. You might confuse them with shale or mudstone but, once again, you are not interested in collecting either of these.

This leaves us with glass pebbles which, unfortunately, do not look at all like the bottle glass from which they.

were formed. Whether clear or coloured, they will be dramatically changed. All glassiness will have disappeared and they will have a frosted, crystalline appearance—very much like pure quartz or some colourful semi-precious pebbles almost unfindable in Britain. The coloured ones are almost certain to be glass, but if you feel lucky break off a tiny fragment with your file. If an obvious glassiness is seen where the fragment has been removed, then glass it is. The colourless pebble could be pure quartz as such pebbles are to be found occasionally on some British beaches. You will be unable to break off a fragment with knifeblade or file if it is quartz. In this case take it home and in a dark room strike it with the blade of your knife. If it sparks and emits a burning vegetable smell you have a valuable quartz pebble.

Incidentally, glass pebbles *will* polish in a tumbler if the barrel is filled entirely with such pebbles.

Summary of unsuitable pebbles
  1 Porous sandstone
  2 Granular sandstone
  3 Flaky shale, slate, mudstone or schist
  4 Veined sandstone
  5 Pitted or cracked pebbles
  6 Brick, concrete, earthenware or china
  7 Glass pebbles, unless you load your tumbler with nothing else but these
  8 Finally, remember not to collect overlarge pebbles or pebbles completely regular in size and shape

Grouping the pebbles Now that you know the pebbles to avoid when collecting we can give some consideration to the pebbles which might end up in one of your bags. Most beginners are attracted to a pebble by its colour and this is a fine way to start. It is unnecessary to arrive at a positive identification of each pebble. You need only know its approximate hardness. Bear in mind, however, that pebbles of the same colour do not necessarily have the same hardness and the first thing you must do when picking up specimens is to determine its approximate hardness. This is a simple operation. Take your penknife and scrape the pebble's surface. You may find that it has a coating—a crust of whitish lime or red, black or even green oxide. Remove some of this crust until the true surface appears. Now attempt to scratch this exposed area with your blade. If you cannot scratch it you have a relatively hard pebble which will probably take a good polish. Try marking it with your hard steel file and if this leaves no mark put it in your 'hard' bag.

Fig. 6 Scratching your pebble with a penknife to determine its hardness

If your knifeblade does scratch the surface you have a pebble which is softer than steel. Check once again that it is not sandstone, shale, mudstone, schist or a man-made material. If not, put it in your 'soft' bag. It will polish under the right conditions.

If your pebble is not marked by your penknife blade but you *can* scratch it with your file you have a borderline pebble which should go into your third bag for closer study at home.

This dividing of pebbles into groups of approximately equal hardness is most important in tumble-polishing. Indeed it might be said to be the key to success. Almost all disappointing results can be traced to insufficient attention to the hardness question, so do make quite sure that you carry out the simple tests described above.

There is a scale of hardness known as Moh's Scale which is often quoted in books on geology, minerology and gemology. It provides a convenient means of indicating the relative hardness of one mineral when compared to another, placing diamond at the top of the scale (10) and talc at the bottom (1). Most British beach pebbles worth polishing lie somewhere in the middle of this scale, and your penknife blade (hardness $5\frac{1}{2}$) and your steel file (hardness $6\frac{1}{2}$) provide two very convenient known hardnesses to enable you to group your finds.

Let us assume you have collected a few pounds of pebbles in your 'hard' bag and you now have them spread out on your kitchen table and ready for grinding and

A closer look at your hard pebbles

polishing. Before you put them into the barrel examine each one closely. Many will probably belong to the quartz family and now is a good time to get to know this family more intimately. Half an hour spent identifying and grouping your finds now will repay great dividends in the future, for you will begin to recognize pebbles and be able to name them more readily. However, it is not essential to know any more about your pebbles at this stage than that they are harder than your steel file. If you wish to skip this next section you may do so and your pebbles will still polish well. I include it for those who wish to improve their recognition skills.

Pebbles having *quartz* as their dominant constituent are found on almost every beach in Britain. As you have already demonstrated for yourself, such pebbles are extremely hard. Their differences in colour and appearance are due to varying amounts of other minerals in each pebble and also to the way in which the quartz has formed.

Quartz is solid silica and if it did not crystallize when it solidified it is known as *flint*—a pebble which most readers will readily identify. You will surely have some in your collection. Pick them all out now and notice the variations possible in this humble pebble; grey, brown or black in colour, often appearing translucent yet not being so when held up to strong light. Everyone knows that two flint pebbles struck against each other will produce a spark, but it is not generally known that all quartz pebbles will do the same and often produce bigger and better sparks.

You will probably confuse chert with flint initially because it can look very similar and differs only slightly in composition. The lighter greys and any smoky-yellow specimens in your flints are likely to be chert. (*See* p. 22.)

Quartzite pebbles are also very likely to be included in your collection. They consist of tiny grains of quartz bonded together in solid silica and usually display a very attractive network of patterns. Unlike the sandstone you have rejected, quartzite is extremely hard. This is because the sand grains in quartzite have been subjected to great pressure and heat at some time in the past and have melted and recrystallized and are now held together in a cement of pure silica. Quartzite pebbles are opaque and colour variations include white, yellow and brown, often with mineral tints of blue and purple.

Quartz breccia was formed in a similar way to quartzite but you should have no difficulty in identifying pebbles of breccia. They consist of angular fragments of rock bonded together in a silica cement. These angular fragments are large enough to see easily and you should rely for identification on this distinctive characteristic since colour variations can be wide. The other pebble which is often confused with breccia is the *conglomerate* (see page oo), but a close look at the rock fragments which make up the pebble will decide the issue. The fragments in a conglomerate will be rounded (like tiny pebbles themselves) and not angular as in breccia.

Milky quartz pebbles should not be difficult to distinguish from flint and chert because they are much lighter in colour (white, creamy yellow) and often translucent or nearly so. They are more likely to be confused with *banded crystalline quartz* which can be white to light brown. Look for multi-coloured patterns and bands. Milky quartz does not have them, banded crystalline quartz does.

If you have been lucky enough to find *agate* pebbles (*see* p. 23.) you will recognize them by their characteristic and very defined banding and their wide colour range— pink, red, yellow, white, brown and blue. Your file test will have already shown that agates are very hard over their entire surface, unlike veined pebbles which are softer between the veins; you will be delighted with any you polish. Disappointment might come later when you try to decide which of the varieties of agate you have found. They are grouped according to colour and banding but there is a certain overlapping of groups which can be confusing. For determined readers bent on positive identification the main groups are:

Banded agate: bands of colour which are parallel to the outer surface

Fig. 7(a) Banded agate

Plate 1 Pebbles which do not polish well

Quartzite   Fine-grained sandstones   Quartz vein in quartzite
Torridonian sandstone   Garnets in mica schist

Plate 2 Flint and chert in a variety of forms

Plate 3 Good polishing pebbles

White quartz	Citrine	Brown jasper
Brown beach agate	Green and Yellow jasper	Whitby jet
Granite	Granite	Rock crystal

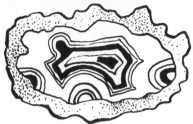

Fig. 7(b) Fortification agate

Fig. 7(c) Eyed agate

Fig. 8 Quartz crystals from Cornwall, magnified × 1½

Eyed agate: bands in concentric rings
Fortification agate: angular bands
Onyx: straight, alternating bands of colour and white
Sardonyx: bands of white and red or brown

If any pebbles suspected of being glass which you have picked up pass your hardness test they may be *clear quartz* (rock crystal). Test them further by striking two pieces together in darkness. They should produce an orange spark and a smell of burning. Perfect quartz crystals are six-sided with a six-sided pyramid at each end, but your chances of finding such specimens on a British beach are remote. Content yourself with very small, frosted pebbles which will reveal their true beauty when tumbled.

Coloured varieties of rock crystal are to be found occasionally on certain beaches. The best-known varieties are:

Amethyst: transparent to semi-transparent; purple to pale pink, with some white banding (*see* p. 26)
Citrine: transparent to semi-transparent; golden yellow (*see* p. 23)
Smoky quartz: transparent to semi-transparent; deep yellow to brown

A variety of quartz which did not form large crystals when it cooled is known as *chalcedony*. It has a waxy lustre, is translucent, and has a milky-white, blue, grey or pale brown colour. It might be confused with milky quartz, but its waxiness should easily distinguish it if the two are compared when dry. The red variety, *cornelian*, is extremely beautiful when polished. These pebbles seem to glow with warm fire when held up to the light and soon catch the eye on a sunny day near the water's edge. Colours vary from pale to deep red and some impure varieties may be speckled and not wholly translucent. Sometimes iron-stained quartz pebbles are mistaken for cornelian but they lack the characteristic waxy feel and translucent warmth.

You must be very careful of the beginner's mistake of assuming that all pebbles can be neatly allocated to a particular group or variety; that each will display one set of characteristics (as set out above) which will allow you to say, 'this is X, Y, or Z' with certainty. Nature did not make her pebbles for the benefit of the collector or tumble-polisher, and many of your quartz pebbles will resist all your efforts to positively identify them. Content yourself with the knowledge that they qualify as 'hard' and will polish well.

The previous paragraph serves as a good introduction to four pebbles requiring special attention: jaspers, conglomerates, porphyritic pebbles and granites. All four will probably find their way into your 'hard' bag at some time during your collecting expeditions and they have much in common.

You are nearly certain to have *jasper* pebbles in your 'hard' bag because they are to be found on almost every

Fig. 9 *Left* a six-sided piece of clear quartz, *centre* a similar piece which has been sea-worn for about 10,000 years, *right* what a tumble-polisher can do in three weeks

Plate 4 Rough British pebbles

Green quartz   Serpentine   Yellow quartz
Obsidian   Amethyst   Red jasper
                       Cornelian

Plate 5 The polished versions

Green quartz   Serpentine   Yellow quartz
Obsidian   Amethyst   Red jasper
             Cornelian

beach in Britain. Jasper consists of tiny quartz grains intermingled with clay which has become coloured by iron salts. Although a very ordinary pebble, it can look beautiful when polished and makes up into charming jewellery. By far the most common single-colour variation is a deep red, and you should always suspect any deep red, opaque pebble of being jasper. Less common colours are yellow and green, sometimes with ribbons of clear quartz running through the pebble. Many jaspers will possess a combination of all three colours and they can be confused with conglomerates. However, jasper pebbles do not usually have the multi-colouring of conglomerates. (*See* pp. 23, 26 & 27.)

Because it is a very common pebble, jasper is one of the first which beginners recognize readily and the temptation to drop all jasper pebbles into the 'hard' bag is difficult to resist, particularly on days when you are in a hurry or the weather is unfriendly. This can lead to problems when tumble-polishing because jasper can fluctuate in hardness. If you have a high percentage of very hard quartz pebbles in the tumbling mixture the softer jasper might break down and upset the process.

The same can be said of *conglomerates*. These pebbles are made up of rounded fragments of a variety of rocks (some of which may be quartz) cemented together in a finely-textured matrix. They are usually quite beautiful and

Summary of hard pebbles

Name	Characteristics
Flint	Opaque to semi-translucent; grey, brown or black
Chert	Opaque to semi-translucent; light grey to smoky-yellow
Quartzite	Opaque. White, yellow, brown, often with a network of patterns and tints of blue or purple. Minute quartz grains in a hard matrix
Quartz breccia	Opaque. Wide colour variations. Angular rock fragments bounded together in a silica matrix

28

multi-coloured but fluctuations in hardness are possible.

Porphyritic pebbles are also formed from a variety of rocks but unlike conglomerates, which have rounded fragments, and quartz breccias, which have angular fragments, these pebbles consist of perfect crystals of quartz and feldspar bounded together in a hard matrix. Once again, different hardnesses are possible.

Finally *granite*. These pebbles are so widespread that you must come across them when collecting. They are composed of three minerals—quartz, feldspar and mica—and vary in colour from grey to pink. The sparkle in granite is caused by particles of mica, while the pink tints are imparted to the pebble by its feldspar content. Variations in hardness are common. (*See* p. 23.)

How then can you decide what to do with these four difficult pebbles? There are three possibilities:

1 Reject them all and stick to pure quartz—an unhappy decision because some of the most beautiful beach pebbles belong to this group.
2 Check each pebble very carefully by trying to scratch its surface in different spots—a better solution, especially if only you have a few specimens.
3 Tumble jaspers, conglomerates, porphyritic pebbles and granite together and keep the purer quartz pebbles apart—the best solution, particularly if you have a tumbler with more than one barrel.

Sometimes confused with	*Tumble with*
Chert	Other quartz pebbles
Flint, limestone	Other quartz pebbles
Conglomerates of similar hardness; jasper, quartz breccia	Other quartz pebbles
Quartzite, conglomerates of similar hardness, jasper porphyritic pebbles, grit	Other quartz pebbles

Fig. 10 Quartz breccia

Name	Characteristics
Milky quartz	Translucent or semi-translucent. White to creamy yellow
Banded crystalline quartz	Opaque to semi-translucent. White to light brown with coloured patterns or bands
Agate	Characterized by strong banding and wide colour range
Clear quartz	Transparent. Pure silica. Colour variations: amethyst, citrine, smoky quartz
Chalcedony	Translucent and waxy. Milky white, blue, grey, pale brown
Cornelian	Translucent and waxy. Pale to deep red
Jasper	Opaque. Deep red, yellow, green, combinations of these—sometimes with ribbons of clear quartz
Conglomerates	Opaque and multi-coloured. Consists of rounded fragments of rock cemented together
Porphyritic pebbles	Opaque. Crystals of quartz and feldspar bounded together in hard matrix
Granite	Opaque. Grey to pink with a sparkle caused by mica particles

...netimes confused with	Tumble with
...anded crystalline quartz, ...nestone	Other quartz pebbles
...ilky quartz	Other quartz pebbles
...ny veined pebble	Other quartz pebbles
...lass	Other quartz pebbles
...ilky quartz	Other quartz pebbles
...on-stained quartz pebbles	Other quartz pebbles
...onglomerates, brick, quartz-...e, quartz breccia, serpentine	Ideally with other jaspers, but can be tumbled satisfactorily with conglomerates, pophyritics, and harder granites. Very hard specimens with other quartz pebbles
...asper, quartzite, quartz brec-...ia, serpentine	Ideally with other conglomerates, but can be tumbled with jasper, porphyritics, and harder granites. Very hard specimens with other quartz pebbles
...Quartz breccia	Ideally with other porphyritics, but can be tumbled with jasper, conglomerates, and harder granites. Very hard specimens with other quartz pebbles
	With other granites unless *very* hard and then best with softer jasper, conglomerates and porphyritics

A closer look at your soft pebbles

A few hours spent hunting pebbles on most British beaches reveals that the vast majority of pebbles fall into two categories—very hard, or too soft. Nevertheless, there is a small but important category somewhere between these two extremes which includes some beautiful specimens. They are soft—but not too soft. With care they can be tumble-polished successfully and the results more than justify their special treatment. One or two in this group are confined to short stretches of coast and this fact can help greatly when you are trying to identify them. But do bear in mind that all pebbles wander far from their birthplace.

One of the best known of the soft pebbles is *serpentine*. It is probably best identified by its feel to your fingers—a soapy, almost lubricated surface which immediately suggests softness. It is an opaque pebble and its main colour variations are pale to dark green and dark red to brown, all with a mottled appearance and sometimes white veins. These might be confused with conglomerates or jasper on appearance but their feel is unique and they are, of course, much softer. (*See* pp. 26 & 27.)

The best location for pebbles of serpentine is The Lizard area of Cornwall, but pebbles can be found on many beaches. If you are collecting in an abundant area such as The Lizard it is a good plan to collect sufficient pebbles to load one of your barrels entirely with serpentine, especially if you are able to find a wide colour range. If you can find only a few pebbles of serpentine they *will* polish with limestone and marble.

Limestone found in Britain is often formed from the skeletons of plants, shells and sea urchins which inhabited these islands millions of years ago and you will often find limestone pebbles which, when polished, will reveal tiny fossils of these organisms. Unfortunately limestone varies greatly in hardness; chalk (a kind of limestone) is too soft for tumble-polishing, but some crystalline limestone can be polished in this way. Best results are probably achieved, by polishing limestone pebbles from a limited area together, but the pebbles *will* polish with marble and serpentine. Limestone pebbles are opaque and can be dull white to yellow, sometimes with colourful staining. They can be confused with milky quartz and chert but are much softer than quartz and will effervesce when a weak acid such as vinegar is applied to their surface.

Marble is limestone which has been subjected to great pressure and heat. It is opaque and has a granular appearance, a crystalline sparkle and a wide colour range. Although soft it is compact and polishes well. Again, best results are achieved by loading the barrel entirely with marble, but it will polish with other soft pebbles.

Incidentally, it is worth remembering that fairly round pebbles of limestone and marble are likely to be harder (and therefore more suitable for polishing) than flattened pebbles which were easily worn by wave action.

Jet is very localized in its distribution, the only good collecting area being the coast around the Yorkshire holiday resort of Whitby. A few pebbles have drifted southward as far as Suffolk but finds are rare. Even around Whitby fair-sized jet pebbles are difficult to find nowadays, but a diligent search should still reveal a few specimens.

Jet is not a stone, but is in fact fossilized wood, similar to, but much tougher than, coal. It is opaque, intense black in colour and very light in weight. If you find a pebble you think is jet, test its weight against a piece of glass of similar size. Your jet pebble should be much lighter. If it is, you may still be confusing jet with a water-worn piece of coal. Sea-coal, as it is known locally, is collected from beaches as fuel only a few miles north of Whitby on the Durham coast and many coal pebbles have drifted south to Yorkshire. Once you have compared a jet pebble with a coal pebble you will easily recognize jet's superior glassiness and greater hardness, but caution is necessary until you have become familiar with it. (*See* p. 23.)

There are certain destructive tests for jet which include setting fire to a specimen. Jet will burn with a greenish flame and a pleasant, tarry aroma, but I do not recommend such tests. Sea-coal has a similar smell when burning and I have seen green flames in a fire made with sea-coal. It is better to rely on appearance for identification and risk mistakes than to see a valuable piece of semi-precious jet go up in smoke. Jet is becoming rare and it will take many days to collect sufficient pebbles to load even a small barrel, but if you are lucky and find enough pebbles their beauty when polished will repay all your efforts.

Amber, like jet, is of a vegetable origin and, again like jet, is very localized in distribution. The coasts of Norfolk and Suffolk are most likely to yield amber, though it has been found on Yorkshire and Essex beaches. It is fossilized tree resin which has been carried to the east coast of England by tides and currents from the Baltic. It is very light in weight and will float in a strong saline solution. Opaque to semi-translucent, amber varies in colour from dark red to pale yellow. Occasionally pieces are found containing fossilized insects. Tests for amber include rubbing a suspected piece vigorously on your sleeve and holding the pebble over small scraps of paper. The scraps will fly upwards towards the pebble, attracted by static electricity. Amber is also very soft, and when scraped with a knife blade will powder readily. It can be confused with similar coloured glass, but is of course much softer. Some plastics, not likely to be found on beaches, are very similar in appearance to amber.

Your chances of finding sufficient amber to load a barrel are almost nil, but it can be polished with jet.

It is worth mentioning that *fossils* are often found when

Summary of soft pebbles	Name	Characteristics
	Serpentine	Opaque. Soapy, lubricated fee Pale to dark green, and dark red brown—all with a mottled appea ance and occasionally white veinin
	Limestone	Opaque. Dull white to yellov sometimes with colourful stainin In the harder, crystalline limeston a sparkle is characteristic. Th softer limestones often reveal foss remains. Effervesces with a wea acid

collecting beach pebbles. Indeed, some pebbles are composed entirely of fossils (*see* limestone). Their hardness depends on the mineral which has replaced the animal or plant. If it was silica the fossil might be seen as a pattern in hard flint or chert pebbles; if limestone, then the pebbles will be softer, though equally beautiful. Fossils could, therefore, find their way into any of your three collecting bags.

Fig. 11 Fossils in limestone. The fossils are likely to be found as small pieces on a beach, especially on the East Coast

Sometimes confused with	*Tumble with*
Conglomerates and jasper	Ideally with other serpentine but can be tumbled successfully with limestone and marble.
Milky quartz, chert	Ideally with limestone pebbles from the same area. Can be tumbled with serpentine and marble

Name	Characteristics
Marble	Limestone which has been su jected to pressure and heat. Opaq granular, with a crystalline spar and wide colour range
Jet	Opaque. Intense glossy blac Confined almost exclusively to t Whitby area of Yorkshire
Amber	Opaque. Semi-translucent. P yellow to dark red
Fossils	See text

A closer look at what is left

No two pebbles are exactly alike. There are always minute differences in hardness and mineral content which make every pebble unique. This is particularly true of the pebbles we are about to examine. Because they are very common pebbles and you are certain to find them they are worthy of some attention in spite of the fact that they are not particularly colourful.

I dismissed sandstone earlier because sandstone pebbles are too soft for tumble-polishing. But pebbles of *grit* are a type of sandstone, yet they are very hard. The grains of sand in pebbles of grit are coarse and angular. A well-known example is *Millstone grit*, once very popular as grinding stones for windmills. The pebbles of this rock differ widely in hardness but you should be able to identify them by looking closely for the coarse, angular grains of which they are composed. Colours are usually dull grey or brown. They might be confused with quartz breccia.

Dolerite is another common pebble and, like grit, it is

Name	Characteristics
Grit	Opaque. Coarse, angular grain Dull grey or brown

Sometimes confused with	Tumble with
	Other marble pebbles or limestone
...a-coal, glass	Probably better to polish by hand
...oloured glass, plastic	Jet, but probably better to polish by hand
	Probably better to polish by hand

dull brown, sometimes with a greenish tinge. It too is composed of grains but they are much finer than those of grit. Tiny crystals of feldspar can also be seen in the pebbles when examined closely. Dolerite is of volcanic origin and is quite hard.

A pebble very similar in origin to dolerite is *whinstone*. It too has crystals of feldspar, but differs in colour, being dark grey to dark blue.

Gabbro is similar to dolerite but has somewhat coarser grains.

Basalt pebbles are pieces of solidified lava which cooled quickly to form dark, iron-black rock.

Finally, *gneiss*—a highly crystalline rock which derives it name from a German word meaning 'to sparkle'. It is composed of bands of quartz, feldspar, and mica—but in spite of its banded appearance (like schist) it can be very hard.

Sometimes confused with	Tumble with
Quartz breccia	Varies in hardness so much that it is probably best not to polish it with other pebbles

Name	Characteristics
Dolerite	Opaque. Fine grained with tir crystals of feldspar. Dull brow sometimes with a green tinge
Gabbro	Very similar to dolerite but coars grained
Basalt	Opaque. Compact, solidified lav Black
Gneiss	Opaque. Highly crystalline pebbl of banded quartz, feldspar, an mica

Note: There are other pebbles to be found on British beach which have not been mentioned in this chapter. They are eith quite rare or foreign pebbles transported to these shores during th Ice Age or as ballast in ships' holds. If you find one, apply th hardness tests and act accordingly.

sometimes confused with	_Tumble with_
Gabbro	Your hard pebbles, if it passes the file test
Dolerite	Varies in hardness. Probably best alone
Black glass	Your hard pebbles, if it passes the file test
schist	Your hard pebbles, it it passes the file test

3 Tumble-polishing machines

Although you may not yet have seen a man-made tumbling machine, you have certainly seen Nature's tumbler at work if you have stood on a beach and watched the rhythmical forces which are constantly at work near the water's edge. Waves breaking on the shoreline cascade their energies up onto the sloping sands. With each wave fragments of rock are rolled up the beach and down again as the energy of each wave is spent, to be caught by the succeeding wave and rolled up once more in a never-ending cycle which carries them up, down and along the beach in a series of gentle arcs. Gradually, relentlessly, these rock fragments are transformed to smooth, round pebbles by the abrasive action of the countless grains of sand over which they roll. A single pebble may be many years in the making, but the sea never stops and the grains of sand are always there and slowly, certainly, each pebble is formed. A thousand years from now those same rhythmical forces which produced it will have reduced it to sand grains

How they work

It is this very same wearing-down-to-smoothness process which a tumble-polishing machine is designed to reproduce and speed up. Instead of the irresistible force of breaking waves, its energy derives from a small electric motor which turns rollers on which a barrel containing pebbles is placed. Inside the barrel silicon carbide grits take the place of sands on the beach. As the barrel revolves these grits wear down the roughened surfaces on each pebble to perfect smoothness. That which Nature takes years to achieve with waves and sand, the tumbling machine can produce in a matter of days. And unlike the sand on a beach, the grits in the tumbler can be carefully graded from very coarse to exceedingly fine. This means that the wearing down process can be controlled and the smoothing process carried to a degree of perfection quite impossible to achieve with sand grains.

Even the gleaming beauty of a sea-washed pebble can be improved upon by the machine. Polishing agents, intro-duced into the barrel during the final stages of the process, impart a mirror-finish to each pebble which makes wet beach pebbles look quite dull by comparison. And unlike wet beach pebbles, which lose their shine as soon as they dry out, correctly tumble-polished pebbles retain their gleaming beauty forever.

The first step on the road to perfect tumble-polishing is to acquire an efficient and reliable tumbling machine. The machines come in a wide variety of shapes and sizes; making the right choice at the outset can be tricky without some knowledge of the way in which the machine works and the job which each component in the machine must do.

A typical tumble-polisher consists of an electric motor which drives a pulley connected via a belt or some other method of drive to one of two parallel rollers. On these rollers a barrel containing the stones to be polished and a suitable abrasive or polish is made to revolve at a pre-determined speed for a number of days. During this period the abrasives in the barrel are changed at regular intervals, each change being to a finer abrasive, until the polishing stage is reached and the pebbles are ready for making into jewellery.

The whole process takes several days and during that time the electric motor must run continuously. A twenty-day cycle, for example, requires 480 hours non-stop running on the part of the motor. It is of the utmost importance, therefore, that the motor is reliable.

The right machine

Fig. 12 The working parts of a tumble-polisher

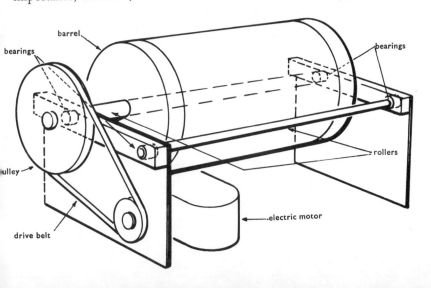

barrel

bearings

bearings

pulley

rollers

drive belt

electric motor

The pulley and belt which transfer the driving power from the motor to the rollers must also be designed to withstand continuous running. A barrel of stones is a heavy load and the job of turning it must be within the capabilities of these components. If other methods of transferring the power of the motor to the rollers are employed, they must be reliable and guarantee positive turning of the rollers at all times during operation.

Rollers and the bearings in which they run must also be designed and built to withstand the toughest wear. The rollers must be capable of withstanding all the friction of a continuously turning barrel of stones and must be of a material which does not allow the barrel to slip as it turns. At the same time they must not in any way prevent free rotation. Bearings are of the utmost importance whatever type or size of machine is considered. They must be tough enough to take long periods of hard work and be designed to allow free roller action. Lubrication must be a simple and straightforward job and must not require dismantling of the machine in order to carry out this essential maintenance.

Finally, we must consider the barrel which probably does more hard work than all the other components put together. A barrel constructed from inferior or non-hardwearing materials will never stand up to the rigours of stone-polishing. It might just be possible to get away with second best on other components but if the barrel has the slightest defect it will certainly be revealed very quickly in use. As will be explained later, water must always be present during the tumbling process and if the barrel is not watertight trouble will soon develop. A leak will certainly impair the efficiency of the rollers if they become wet, and there is a danger of an electrical fault if any leaking water finds its way to the motor. The lid of the barrel must also be wide enough to allow easy entry and exit of the pebbles and your hand because you will be putting pebbles in and taking them out many times during the barrels's working life. You will also be cleaning the barrel regularly so it must be designed in a way that eliminates corners and angles difficult to reach when washing out used abrasives. If even a few grains of a coarse abrasive are allowed to remain in the barrel during any subsequent stage in the polishing sequence the result will be an inferior finish to the final polish. Easy-to-clean, therefore, should be high on your list of points to look for when making your choice.

To summarize: A good tumble-polishing machine must

1 have a reliable motor
2 have a strong pulley and drive belt, or other driving method
3 have tough, hard-wearing rollers
4 have efficient bearings
5 be easy to lubricate and maintain
6 have a strong, leak-proof, easy-to-clean barrel.

In spite of the rigorous specifications outlined above, it does not follow that a good tumbler must be built like a battleship. Good design and the choice of lightweight but durable materials can greatly reduce cost, weight and wear. If a manufacturer has achieved low cost and light weight and is prepared to guarantee his machine against defects for any reasonable length of time, he is likely to be marketing a sound product.

There are many makes, types and sizes of machine on the market and the best advice I can offer you before buying is to keep the above points in mind and buy from a reliable supplier. Such a supplier will *always* guarantee his machine against any of the faults outlined above and give you the benefit of his experience if you call at his premises.

Many readers will be buying their machines by post and it is advisable to write to three or four suppliers initially asking for catalogues and price lists. The less expensive tumblers will not necessarily be the best, but you should be able to check on most of the points already mentioned by comparing catalogues. Incidentally, no reader should worry greatly about ordering by post. The vast majority of mail order firms in the lapidary busineess are very reliable and most sell on a refund-if-not-delighted basis.

Barrel size: The size of the barrel or barrels on your tumbling machine predetermines a surprising number of things about the pebbles you can put into it. For a start, it determines the amount of pebbles you can polish at once. It is physically impossible to put ten pounds of pebbles into a barrel with a capacity of three pounds.

Secondly, it determines the size of pebbles you can polish in the barrel. A small barrel will not polish large pebbles.

Thirdly, it determines the amount of abrasive grits and polishing powder you need to carry out the process. A very large barrel needs more grits and polish than does a very small barrel.

Fourthly, because the barrel—whatever its size—must be filled to a predetermined level with pebbles, the amount of pebbles you must *collect* before you can start the operation has also been decided once you choose a particular size of barrel.

Fig. 13 A small tumbler with a single
1½-lb barrel

44

Let us now look at five typical tumble-polishing machines with barrels of different sizes and consider their relative merits:

1. *A small tumbler with a single one-and-a-half pound barrel:* This little machine will be quite inexpensive and will do a lot of work. Its barrel will hold approximately 100 pebbles ranging in size from equal to your little fingernail up to the size of the top joint of your thumb. It will be very economical on grits and polish and you should have no difficulty in finding enough pebbles to fill it during an hour's stroll along a good shingle beach.

Its disadvantages are:

(a) if you have collected both hard and soft pebbles and filled the barrel with the hard ones you will have to wait approximately three weeks before you can make a start on the soft ones;

(b) you will not be able to polish pebbles larger than the sizes mentioned above;

(c) if you have collected several pounds of pebbles, it will take many weeks to polish them all.

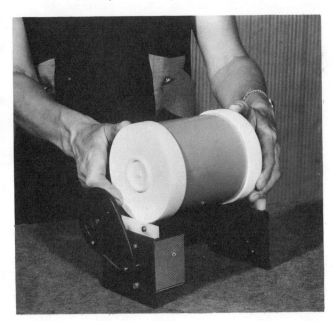

Fig. 14 A tumbler with a single 3-lb barrel

2. *A small tumbler with a single three-pound barrel:* Although slightly more expensive, this little machine will do twice the work of No. 1. You will be able to polish 200 or so pebbles at once and you will be able to include half a dozen slightly larger pebbles.

Its disadvantages are:

(*a*) once again you will have to wait three weeks between each batch of hard and soft pebbles;

(*b*) you will have to collect 200 pebbles before you can start the process. This is not difficult in summer when weekend trips to the coast are a regular feature of family life, but it is worth bearing in mind as winter approaches.

3. *A larger tumbler with two one-and-a-half pound barrels:* This twin-barrelled model has the advantage of a total capacity of approximately 200 pebbles, but what is more important is its ability to do two jobs at once. You can load one barrel with hard pebbles, the other with soft, and three weeks later they are all ready for making into jewellery. As will be explained in the chapter on polishing

Fig. 15 A tumbler with two 1½-lb barrels

pebbles, there are certain advantages in keeping one barrel
solely for use in the final polishing stage of the process.
With this machine you can do that and still have your
second barrel working on grinding other pebbles.

The only disadvantage worth mentioning with this
machine is that you are, of course, limited on pebble
size to the requirements of a one-and-a-half pound barrel.

4. *A larger tumbler with one three-pound barrel and two
one-and-a-half pound barrels:* This is a de-luxe machine with
the single disadvantage of being fairly expensive. However,
its advantages more than justify its greater cost. Total
capacity is around 400 pebbles, but if you happen to be low
on supplies you don't have to wait until you can get down
to the beach again. Simply use one of the small barrels as
you would with No. 1 above. If you have a good stock of
pebbles you can add some larger ones when using the three-
pound barrel; you can keep one of the small barrels just for
polishing; you can put three pounds of pebbles through
the first and second grinding stages and then carefully
select the best of the batch to fill one of your one and a half
pounders. Indeed, a very versatile machine.

47

5. A very large tumbler with a twelve-pound barrel: This giant will polish 800 pebbles in one cycle, enough to keep the average home jewellery maker going for many months. As the barrel must be filled with either hard or soft

Summary

Tumbler capacity	Barrels
1½lb	One, taking approximately 1(pebbles
3lb	One, taking approximately 200 pebbles
3lb	Two, taking approximately 1(pebbles each
6lb	Three, one taking approximatel) 200 pebbles two taking approx mately 100 pebbles each
12lb	One, taking approximately 8(pebbles

Anyone contemplating starting a business in tumble-polishing stones is recommended to give large tumblers careful consideration. Similarly, their ability to polish quite large pebbles must not be overlooked. If you plan to use pebbles for projects other than jewellery-making and you need large quantities of bigger pebbles, a big barrel is likely to be your choice.

But whatever your choice—large, small or in-between—I advise you strongly against metal barrels unless they are adequately lined on the inside with hardwearing rubber. Chemical reactions which produce gas can be set up in an unlined metal barrel if it is filled with pebbles, water and abrasive and made to revolve for any length of time on a pebbles you will need 1600 pebbles in stock, almost too many unless you are going in for jewellery-making on a commercial scale. It will, of course, polish much larger pebbles than any of the four previously mentioned.

dvantages	Disadvanatages
expensive; easy to fill; very onomical on grits and polish	Can only tumble one load of hard or soft pebbles in one three-week cycle; limitation on pebble size
Vill take *some* larger pebbles	Can only tumble one load of hard or soft pebbles in one three-week cycle
'an polish hard and soft pebbles t the same time in separate arrels	Limitations on pebble size
'xtremely versatile; large total apacity, but can also be used or tumbling small loads. Can rind hard and soft pebbles, and olish a third batch at the same me	More expensive than any above
Vill polish larger pebbles. Ideal or commercial use	Difficult to fill owing to large capacity; can only tumble one load of hard or soft pebbles in one three-week period. Expensive

machine. The gas, usually hydrogen, is produced by a reaction of the acids normally present in water and pebbles with the particles of metal which are removed from the inside of the barrel by abrasion. The danger from explosions is negligible, but the possibility of the lids being forced off or seams failing under pressure is quite high in an unlined metal barrel. The mess which results from a lid coming off a barrel unexpectedly is a quite sufficient reason for avoiding such barrels. If you *must* use metal, make absolutely sure that the lining seals off as much of the inner surface of the barrel as is possible from contact with grits, water and pebbles.

Plastic barrels are almost problem-free as far as gas is

concerned. There is no reaction between acids and metal in plastic barrels and the small amount of gas which is generated by grinding pebbles in water is dissipated when the lid is removed for regular inspection of the pebbles during the polishing process. Some recently introduced barrels have safety valves built in to provide a suitable gas vent.

The final point I wish to make about choosing a tumbler applies to all models, whatever their size or method of construction. Remember that all machines are subject to wear. There will come a time when a component needs replacing or the whole machine needs servicing. At such times it is comforting to know that your supplier can help; that he has in stock any replacement part you need. If you buy a tumbler made in Timbuktu you will probably have to take or send it back to Timbuktu if a fault develops. If, on the other hand, the manufacturer can be reached quickly by letter or telephone you will have few problems when the need for servicing arises.

Home-made and more advanced machines

It would be unfair to close this chapter without a brief reference to home-made tumblers and more sophisticated machines now being developed for the hobby market. Many mechanically-minded enthusiasts have made their own tumble polishing machines and produced excellent polished pebbles. But it is not a project to be undertaken lightly. Pulley sizes, belt length, speed or rotation and size of barrel must all be carefully calculated if a home-made machine is going to be a success. Unless you are accustomed to tackling such design problems or you can enlist the help of a knowledgeable friend, I would advise against a home-made job. You can buy a small but very efficient tumbler complete with electric motor and ready to go for less than ten pounds. You might save half of that sum if you made your own successfully. An excellent book for those contemplating making their own tumbling machine is *Gem Tumbling and Baroque Jewellery Making* by The Victors, available from lapidary shops.

The next generation of tumble-polishers are likely to have many new design features to make the job of achieving a perfect polish much easier. I have already mentioned other methods of driving the rollers, and barrels with gas vents. Other new ideas include variable speed drives which can make the rather difficult job of achieving a good polish on softer pebbles much simpler. The barrel can be slowed down during critical periods such as polishing and the final result can be carefully controlled. No doubt, these new machines will cost a little more than conventional tumblers; but for readers seeking easier methods of achieving perfection they are worth considering.

Fig. 17 The 'Vari-speed' tumbler, which can be adjusted to turn faster or slower according to the kind of pebbles you are tumbling

4 Perfect polishing

We have now arrived at the exciting moment when you start to polish. You have collected several pounds of pretty pebbles; perhaps even learned the names of and begun to recognize the more interesting ones; and you have bought yourself a tumbler and a supply of grits and polish. You are ready to start.

The first important question to settle is where you are going to keep your machine. It makes a certain amount of noise so I do not recommend a bedroom unless you are a heavy sleeper. Take a handful of pebbles and pour them from one hand to the other half a dozen times. That should give you some idea of the noise you will get from the machine when you start tumbling.

Next you should consider where you least mind a bit of mess. Remember you will be filling and emptying the barrels with pebbles, water, grits and polish many times during the machine's life.

Finally, has the spot you have selected a nearby electrical point where you can safely plug in your machine? You do not want yards of cable lying around for other members of the family to trip over. You should find a place at about table-top height where you can get at the machine comfortably to change grits, inspect barrels, oil bearings, and generally fuss over the thing without getting in anyone's way.

I suppose most tumblers are set to work in a quiet corner of the kitchen and if you can find such a spot it should prove ideal. Spread out a dozen sheets of newspaper and stand your tumbler on them. A sheet at a time can be removed during cleaning-up operations and they will also help reduce noise by cushioning vibrations when the barrel is turning. You can fit a three-pin plug at this stage. Make quite sure you wire it correctly and make the earth connection. Tumblers are perfectly safe to run from the household electricity supply but remember you are using water in the process. To disregard safety measures which the manufacturer has built into the machine would be very foolish.

For the purpose of writing this chapter I have assumed

that you have bought a tumbler similar to the six-pound model with one three-pound and two one-and-a-half pound barrels described in the previous chapter. If you have bought a different model you will find that the basic polishing process is the same with all machines and I have added notes where necessary to guide owners of smaller or larger machines. The one I have chosen has the advantage of versatility and incorporates both small and fairly large barrels so much of what follows will apply to everyone.

Grits and polish

We will have a closer look at these. Silicon carbide is a man-made abrasive substance which is extremely hard. You will remember the reference to Moh's Scale in the chapter on selecting pebbles (see p. 19). Silicon carbide has a hardness of more than 9·5 on that scale and is many, many times harder than the toughest pebble in your 'hard' bag. It also has the advantage of forming, when made, into wedge-shaped grains, which makes it an excellent grinding material.

When manufactured by heating and then crushing a mixture of silica sand, carbon, salt and sawdust, it is then graded by being passed through a series of fine mesh

Fig. 18 Grinding and polishing compounds. Densities range from (*left*) very coarse to (*right*) finest polish

screens. The familiar No. 80 grit with which almost all tumble-polishing starts gets its name from the fact that it has passed through a screen with 80 meshes to the inch.

You may have bought two or three grades of silicon carbide, depending on the manufacturer's instructions. The point to bear in mind is that the coarse grit has the *lowest* number and the finer the grit, the higher its grade number. A quick examination of the particles in each container will soon resolve matters if you are in any doubt about which is coarse and which is fine. Some manufacturers recommend mixed grades which gradually break down inside the barrel and these are excellent if the manufacturer's instructions are followed.

The two most common polishes are cerium oxide and tin oxide and you should use whichever the manufacturer recommends. *These are not grinding materials.* Their purpose is to add a permanent polish to the perfectly smooth pebbles you have produced in the earlier stages. No amount of polishing will remove any roughness you allow to remain on your pebbles after grinding. If there *is* roughness you have not ground your pebbles long enough and you will merely waste polish if you do not put matters right by going back to an earlier grinding stage.

Last minute checks

Your tumbler should have reached you in perfect condition, but you should check carefully before you switch on, especially if it reached you by mail. Check that it has been oiled and that the rollers are parallel and there are no obvious signs that the machine has received a severe blow in transit. There should be no loose wires hanging about and the belt should sit squarely in the grooves on the pulleys. If all seems well, plug in and switch on. The drive roller will turn much faster without a load and you should allow the machine to run for a few minutes like this. All moving parts should turn smoothly. If you hear odd scraping noises or if the rollers turn intermittently, something is not as it should be. Switch off at once and check your plug wiring and the manufacturer's instructions. If the machine does run smoothly, we will have a closer look at the barrels.

Take the lid off one of your barrels and look inside. The inner walls should be perfectly smooth. If your barrels are metal and have rubber linings make sure that the lining is correctly fitted and there are no bulges or loose seams. If the lid is fitted with a gasket or rubber seal this too should be correctly seated.

You will have already sorted your pebbles into hard and soft groups so let us start with your hard ones. Go through them once again to seek out any that have slipped through into the wrong bag. Now is the time to discard badly cracked specimens. The first grind is a tough operation and any cracked specimens are unlikely to survive. For a one-and-a-half pound barrel you will need approximately one hundred pebbles, the largest not more than one inch across; the smallest approximately a quarter of an inch. Try to select a range of shapes—ovals, spheres, discs— because the grinding action is more efficient when different shapes are mixed together.

A three-pound barrel will require approximately two hundred pebbles and you will be able to include half a dozen larger specimens—up to a maximum size of two

Loading your barrels

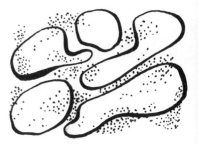

Fig. 19 (a) and (b) A variety of shapes and sizes is the key to success when selecting pebbles or rocks for the tumbler. The small stones grind into the hollows of the large ones

Fig. 20 It is vital that the barrel is
loaded correctly, to about three-
quarters full

inches. Similarly, larger barrels will take more pebbles with
a proportionate number of big ones. All, however, require
a grading of sizes from large to small, with plenty of variety
in shape.

Note that I headed this section, "Loading your barrels"
—*not* filling them. Tumbler barrels must never be filled
as cans of beans are filled. If they are they will never
polish pebbles. The tumbling action depends on there
being sufficient space inside the barrel to allow the pebbles
to fall, one over the next, as the barrel revolves.

Too much space and too few pebbles is quite as bad as
overfilling. If you do not put sufficient pebbles into the
barrel they do not ride up the walls to the point where
tumbling commences. They slide back to the bottom and
all you get out of the barrel are badly polished flattened
discs. So do make a point of getting the amount right.
A little under three-quarters full of pebbles of different
shapes and sizes should be your aim. This applies to any
size of barrel. Place the pebbles inside gently. You spent a
long time selecting perfect specimens and it would be a
pity to crack or scratch them now. Shake the barrel gently
to settle them as you put them in and stop when you near
the three-quarters-full point.

Many books and articles emphasize that tumbling is a mechanical process and that the operator has no control over the finished results. I emphatically disagree with this argument. *You* are in control of the operation from start to finish. You select the pebbles; you decide when they are ready for the next stage; you polish them. You may not see the entire operation, but how well you conduct and control the process determines the quality of the polish you achieve. You should keep this in mind as you proceed. Learn by observation, trial and error the best ways of doing each operation. No book can tell you when a particular batch of pebbles is ready for the next stage. You must learn to judge this by experience, learning all you can from your early mistakes and aiming with each new batch of pebbles to improve on your previous results.

There are two excellent ways in which you can start on this road to success now. The first is to keep back a small selection from each batch of pebbles you put into the barrel. Half a dozen will do. Make sure they are representative of the ones you do polish in collecting location, type, colour and size. Put them into a small box or bag and label it so that you know from which beach you collected them. If you have come across any pebbles you were unable to identify on that particular beach and you wish to know how they will polish, you have only to wait and see. This type of comparison—unpolished pebble with finished result—is worth a hundred coloured illustrations in any book and you will soon be able to recognize those pebbles on a particular beach which polish well. Incidentally if you have more than one barrel and they look alike, stick a strip of adhesive tape or plaster on each lid and number your barrels a, b, c, etc. This will avoid confusion later.

The second helpful suggestion is to keep a simple progress chart so that you can record the dates and times you commence and finish different stages in the process, together with comments on results achieved. This information will prove invaluable when next you polish a batch of similar pebbles and you wish to try variations in grinding and polishing times in an effort to better your previous

A grinding and polishing chart

Description of pebbles. Types, where collected	Barrel number	Days on coarse grind	Days on medium grind
EXAMPLE: Flints, quartzite and agates from beaches around Hastings, Sussex	I	5	4

results. Keeping such records and retaining a few pebbles from each batch for comparisons will very soon lead you to perfection in polishing.

You can work out a log similar to the one above for any make or type of tumbler. Read the manufacturer's instructions first—particularly with regard to the number of stages in progress—and prepare your chart accordingly. A school exercise book suitably ruled makes an excellent log. Hang it up somewhere near the machine and get into the habit of keeping entries up to date. It will prove to be a mine of information during the months ahead.

The first grind

Now that you have loaded your barrel with pebbles you must add the coarse silicon carbide. The amount of grit depends on the barrel's capacity. A one-and-a-half-pound barrel requires a heaped table-spoonful, while a three-pound barrel requires twice that amount. Check the manufacturer's instructions for other barrel sizes and act accordingly. You should never put too much or too little grit into the barrel as this will upset the grinding process. Use a clean, dry spoon to measure the amount required and shake it evenly over the pebbles in the barrel.

It is of the utmost importance that you do not contaminate the grits and polish, especially by getting any of the coarse grit into the finer material or polish. Keep them well apart. If you can find a few old cocoa tins or similar containers they make excellent holders for your materials. Label the tins and keep them out of harm's way.

The next step is to run tap water into the barrel until it

Days on fine grind	Days on polish	Hours on final wash	Results and comments
4	4 Polycel added	6	Good polish Might have been improved by longer medium/fine stages

just covers the top of the pebbles. Don't *fill* the barrel with water. Stop as soon as you see the water cover the pebbles and put the lid on the barrel. You must replace the lid so that it forms a watertight fit on the barrel. Some lids will screw on; other will be a push fit; and some will be fixed by nuts and bolts. All can be prevented from fitting correctly if grains of grit are allowed to remain on the lid or the part of the barrel which comes into contact with the lid. Wipe this area carefully before putting the lid in place and read the manufacturer's instructions for achieving a watertight fit before putting the barrel on the rollers. When you have the lid on, wipe the outside of the barrel to remove water and grit and check that water is not

Fig. 21 Adding the correct amount of silicon carbide

Fig. 22 Remember not to overfill the
tumbler with water. Just make sure
that the pebbles are covered

leaking around the cap. If all is well switch on the tumbler
and place the barrel onto the turning rollers. The rollers
will immediately slow down under the weight of the barrel
but should settle down at once to a steady speed of revolu-
tion. Watch the barrel for a minute or two, checking for
a steady rotation and no water leaks.

Although you cannot see inside the barrel as it turns on
the rollers, you can tell a great deal about what is happening
inside by listening to the sound of the pebbles as they grind.
The pebbles should be tumbling or rolling one over the
next as they near the top of the barrel in a continuous,
rythmical motion. If you have proceeded this far and
followed all the advice given above, that is the gentle,
rolling sound you should hear. If you hear bangs and knocks,
or the sound of pebbles falling and hitting each other,
something is wrong. You have not put sufficient pebbles
into the barrel, or you have put too many of the wrong
size. If you hear little or no movement you have put too
many pebbles into the barrel and the tumbling action is
not operating.

You are about to discover that tumble-polishing requires
a good deal of patience because now you must allow the
barrel to turn on the rollers for the next twenty-four hour
without interruption. This is always difficult for beginners

who find it hard to resist taking the barrel off the rollers every hour or so to see what has happened to their precious pebbles. Very little happens in one hour. But slowly, gradually, your pebbles are being worn to smoothness. When twenty-four hours has passed you can take the barrel off and carefully open the lid. You will probably find it easier to switch off the motor when removing the barrel during the first few days, but you should soon get the knack of lifting the barrel cleanly and neatly from the rollers without stopping the machine—and replacing it just as expertly when you have finished your inspection.

Once the lid is removed you should see a dark grey liquid. Working over the kitchen sink, and with the tap turned on, carefully lift out half a dozen pebbles. Shake off as much of the slurry as possible before moving them clear of the barrel. Put the barrel to one side and run the pebbles you have removed under the tap to wash away all traces of the grey liquid. Now examine the washed pebbles carefully. Already they will feel smoother to your fingers, but they have a long way to go to perfection. Select one of the pebbles and dry it carefully. Now examine it under a good light and you will see the tiny pits and cracks on its surface.

Back into the barrel it must go, along with the others you removed. Wash the lid and the top of the barrel to remove all traces of grit and replace the lid as you did before. Once you are satisfied that you have a watertight seal switch on the tumbler and replace the barrel on the rollers. Again, watch it for a minute or two to check for leaks. If all is well, wait another day and repeat the inspection.

You alone must decide when your pebbles are ready for the next stage. Fairly smooth beach pebbles composed mainly of quartz will take between three and six days to grind to the required smoothness. The aim is to remove all surface blemishes, pits and cracks from every pebble in the barrel, but this perfection is rarely, if ever, achieved. If you continue coarse grinding until the worst pebble in the barrel is perfectly smooth, the remainder will be too much reduced in size. Indeed, the smallest could be ground away completely if you allowed the first stage to go on too long. A compromise is what you should aim for.

When the day comes that four, or possibly five, of the half-dozen pebbles you remove for inspection satisfy you by their smoothness and blemish-free appearance that they are ready, it is time to call a halt. Remove all the pebbles from the barrel and place them in the sink with the tap running. A plastic sink tidy or colander makes an excellent container for the pebbles at this stage. Let the tap run onto them to wash away all traces of grit.

You must not under any circumstances pour the sludge in the barrel down the waste pipe. It will very quickly block your drains and you will be faced with an expensive plumbing job. The best way to dispose of it is to find a suitably-sized plastic bag and carry it, with the barrel, out to the dustbin. Pour the contents of the barrel into the bag and put the bag into the dustbin.

Now, back to the kitchen and wash everything—pebbles, barrel, lid, your hands, and then wash the pebbles again. If you have made a mess around the machine remove one of the sheets of newspaper after cleaning the rollers on the tumbler. Now is probably a good time to lubricate the roller bearings and carry out any other weekly maintenance recommended by the manufacturer.

Fig. 23 The end of the first stage. The pebbles should now be perfectly smooth

Do this before you remove a sheet of newspaper and you will be ship-shape for the next stage in the process.

1 Check your tumbler.
2 Load barrel just less than three-quarters full with suitably sized pebbles.
3 Add correct amount of coarse grit.
4 Add water—just covering pebbles.
5 Clean cap and barrel.
6 Replace cap and check that it is watertight.
7 Switch on tumbler and place barrel on rollers, again checking for leaks.
8 Inspect daily—remember to carry out steps 5 and 6 each time.
9 When pebbles are ready remove them from the barrel.
10 Dispose of sludge in the dustbin.
11 Wash everything very carefully.
12 Carry out machine maintenance.

Quality control

We have now arrived at a point where many beginners fall by the wayside along the path to perfect polishing. The task is simple: dry your pebbles carefully, spread them out on a sheet of newspaper, examine them and reject every one that retains a blemish, pit, or crack. Ruthlessness is what is required and many beginners lack it. They allow poor quality pebbles to slip through to the next stage instead of eliminating them at this stage. When, at the end of the process, they gaze forlornly at the final result they blame the machine, the manufacturer or their own bad luck when all the time the fault is their own. So do be ruthless. The pebbles you reject now can be put back into the barrel when you start your next coarse grind and you will probably be delighted with the result. Meanwhile, put them aside.

This rejection process will of course reduce the bulk of your pebbles by about five or ten per cent. The coarse silicon carbide will also have rendered each pebble smaller

Fig. 24 Quality control. Eliminate badly cracked and pitted pebbles now

in size and the combined effect of rejection and wear will probably reduce the entire batch by up to fifteen per cent of its original volume.

If rejection has been high, or wear very great, and you only have one barrel on your tumbler this can mean that you are unable to load it correctly for the next stage. This ceases to be a problem when you have been tumbling for some time. You will always have odd polished pebbles lying around which for one reason or another you have not made into jewellery, and these can be used as fillers to make up the bulk of the load. If you have a very small, single-barrelled tumbler there are two courses of action you can take if the bulk of your pebbles falls below the minimum two-thirds loading line and you have not built up a stock of polished pebbles from which to draw to make up the load.

1. Put to one side the pebbles you have already processed through the first stage and start again with a new load of pebbles. When this second load has been coarse ground you will have more than enough pebbles to continue to the next stage.

2. Accept that you will not achieve perfection at your first polishing attempt and continue to the second stage

with all the pebbles you have put through the first stage.

If you are lucky enough to have a tumbler with large *and* small barrels and you loaded one of your large barrels to begin with, you will now begin to see the advantages of your machine. Simply load a smaller barrel from the pebbles you have left after rejecting all the cracked and pitted specimens and continue with the next stage.

The second grind

Whichever course you decide upon, the next steps are to check that your tumbler is working correctly, and that your barrel is absolutely clean and free from all traces of coarse grit, then load it once more to just less than three-quarters full with pebbles. Take your container of finer grit, add the correct amount to the barrel and then cover the pebbles with water again. Secure the cap, after carefully cleaning it, and place the loaded barrel onto the rollers once more.

This second stage in the tumbling process is the most important of all. It is also the stage at which many attempts at perfection fail because most beginners are apt to regard it as a grinding process similar to the first grind with coarse grit. But it is much more.

During the first two or three days the fine silicon carbide *does* in fact continue the grinding process begun by the coarse grit. Scratches and tiny imperfections—some of them made by the coarse grit—are gradually worn away. It is at this point that the real work of the second stage begins. The fine grit starts to break down. It loses its power to remove scratches and pit-marks and now prepares the pebble for the final polish. You will see now why there is little to be gained from leaving badly pitted pebbles in the barrel at the end of the first stage. So little grinding takes place during the second stage that any deep imperfections cannot be removed. What you must also see is the importance of continuing the second stage until the pebbles *are* ready for polishing. Be patient. Be prepared, if necessary, to run this stage twice as long as the coarse grind. Your final results really do depend on it.

65

Fortunately, it is quite easy to decide when the pebbles have been long enough in the barrel on this stage. You will, of course, be checking their progress daily by opening the barrel and carefully washing half a dozen pebbles under the tap before examining their surfaces. What you are looking for is absolute smoothness over the entire surface of each pebble. The smallest pit marks will ruin the final polish so examine your samples very, very carefully. At the end of this stage the pebbles should look exactly as they will when polished—except for their lack of shine. A matt-finish probably best describes what you must aim for. When it will come depends on a number of variable factors, but you might begin to expect it five or six days after commencing your second stage. If, on examination, you think that your samples are ready, take a small piece of felt and soak it under the tap. Next, sprinkle a small amount—half a teaspoonful would be more than enough—of your polishing powder onto the wet felt. Take one of your sample pebbles firmly between finger and thumb and rub it vigorously backwards and forwards over the impregnated felt forty or fifty times. Now, carefully dry the area of pebble you have polished and examine it very closely in good light. Look for tiny pinpricks or scratches on the polished surface. If you see even one you must continue the second stage for at least a

Fig. 25 Test-polishing on a piece of felt impregnated with polishing compound

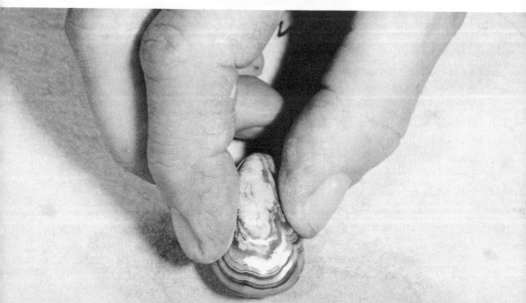

further twenty-four hours before test-polishing another pebble. If you are quite satisfied that the surface you have polished is perfect the second stage is complete.

Incidentally, if you do see tiny pin-pricks or scratches when you examine your sample, do not under any circumstances add more fine grit to the barrel in the hope that you will speed up the process. You will do quite the reverse. After five or six days of second stage tumbling your pebbles are nearing their final smoothness and even fine silicon carbide will scratch them. If you add more grit now you will have to begin the second stage again. The correct procedure is to put the pebbles back into the barrel and continue until you can achieve a perfect polish on the test specimen.

Step by step through the second stage

1 Make sure you have washed away all traces of coarse grit from pebbles, barrel, caps and rollers.
2 Load barrel just less than three-quarters full with selected pebbles from the first run. (Or continue with all pebbles if you have only one barrel and this is your first attempt at polishing.)
3 Add correct amount of fine grit.
4 Add water—just covering pebbles.
5 Clean cap and barrel top.
6 Replace cap and check that it is watertight.
7 Switch on tumbler and place barrel on rollers, again checking for leaks.
8 Inspect daily—remember to carry out 5 and 6 each time.
9 After five or six days, test polish one pebble on a piece of felt impregnated with polishing powder.
10 If satisfactory, remove pebbles carefully from barrel.
11 Dispose of sludge in dustbin.
12 Wash everything very carefully. Take even more care than you did after the first grind.
13 Carry out machine maintenance.

The final polish

You now have a batch of unpolished but perfectly smooth pebbles and your aim should be to impart a mirror-finish to each one. Handle them very carefully at this stage. Don't pour them from one container to another. When washing them to remove every trace of silicon carbide, don't allow them to knock one against the other. The smallest scratch or chip will show up when they are polished, so do handle with care.

Owners of versatile, multi-barrelled tumblers will be able to keep one barrel solely for final polishing without additional expense and, although it means further outlay on equipment, I recommend buying a second barrel for this purpose to owners of single-barrelled machines. If your aim is perfection in polishing, a second barrel is a worthwhile investment because it reduced to nil the chances of odd particles of silicon carbide remaining in the barrel after the second stage has been completed. Very careful washing of the inside of the barrel will do much to prevent this if you must limit expense, but remember that tiny scratches on the barrel's inner surface can trap grit particles which will resist your efforts to remove them with water.

Having made sure that the barrel you are going to use is absolutely clean, place the pebbles carefully inside, one at a time, until you have the required load—that is, just under three-quarters full. There will have been little reduction in volume during the second stage because, as already explained, so little grinding takes place. If you had the correct load at the beginning of the second stage you should have just the right amount now.

Take your container of polishing powder and add the correct amount of polish to the barrel. Cover the pebbles with clean water, replace the cap, make sure that everything is clinically clean and return the barrel to the rollers.

As already pointed out, sound plays an important part in tumble-polishing. During this final stage you should pay particular attention to the sound of your pebbles as they tumble in the barrel. A steady and rhythmical motion inside the barrel will produce the steady and rhythmical sound of pebbles tumbling one over the next. Any harsh banging or unrhythmical striking of pebbles together is a sure sign that the tumbling action is not being carried out. If this is allowed to happen during the polishing stage it will certainly produce cracks and scratches on the pebble's surfaces.

The commonest cause of cracks and scratches at this stage is an insufficient load. With too few pebbles in the barrel the load is thrown about violently, causing one pebble to strike against the next so harshly that cracks and scratches are the inevitable result. This should not happen if you have followed all the advice given so far, but if you do hear any irregular sounds during the first twenty-four hours of the polishing stage you should take remedial action at once.

Remove the barrel from the rollers, take off the lid and add a small amount of wallpaper adhesive to the mixture. The aim is to thicken the liquid in the barrel so that it cushions the fall of each pebble. Do not make the mixture too thick, otherwise the effectiveness of the polishing agent could be reduced. A thin cream consistency is ideal and it is better to err on the side of thinness rather than add too much at the outset. The addition of the paste will, you may notice, reduce the noise your pebbles make as they tumble. It also increases the time you must allow for the polish to do its work because movement inside the barrel is reduced owing to the greater viscosity of the thickened liquid. A polishing stage of four days without paste might take seven days if paste is added.

The noise reduction question is often in the minds of beginners—especially if they live in flats or cannot find an out-of-the-way spot for their machine. The noise is not very considerable and you should never disregard safety or the final results you wish to achieve when considering noise reduction. Do not put your machine into a padded box. The motor will overheat if adequate ventilation is not provided. Pads of rubber or felt under the base of the machine will do almost as much in the way of reducing noise and they will not prevent ventillation. You should regard the noise reduction achieved by the addition of wallpaper paste at the polishing stage as incidental.

The paste is put in to prevent cracking and scratching of the pebbles. Do not, by the way, add paste during the earlier grinding stages in an effort to reduce noise—unless you are prepared to accept very long first and second stages.

Daily inspection of your pebbles is just as important at the polishing stage as it is during grinding so do not neglect it. The process should take from four to seven days to complete and only experience will tell you when the polish has done its work. There comes a time in the process when no amount of further polishing will improve the finish. Indeed, if the barrel were allowed to turn for an excessively long period the final polish would deteriorate. Daily inspection, your log book and experience will guide you on this point. If you examine half a dozen pebbles each day and stop the process on the day you see no improvement on the previous day's polish, your results should be satisfactory.

Step by step through the final polish

1 Double check that all traces of silicon carbide have been removed from your pebbles by thoroughly washing them in running water.
2 Place your pebbles very carefully into the polishing barrel. (If you are using the same barrel it *must* be clinically clean.)
3 Add correct amount of polishing powder.
4 Add water—just covering pebbles.
5 Replace cap and check that all is watertight.
6 Switch on the tumbler and place barrel on rollers, again checking for leaks.
7 If tumbling action sounds harsh add a small amount of wallpaper paste to the barrel.
8 Inspect daily. Remember to carry out 5 each time.
9 When polish cannot be improved upon carefully remove pebbles from barrel.
10 Dispose of sludge in dustbin.
11 Wash everything very carefully.
12 Carry out machine maintenance.

The polishing powder leaves a film on the pebbles which is removed by placing the pebbles in the cleaned barrel, covering with water, and adding not more than half a teaspoonful of detergent to break down the surface tension of the water. Run the barrel for four to eight hours, then remove the pebbles very carefully and wash off the detergent in running water. Place all the pebbles on a soft cloth and allow them to dry.

If you keep a careful log of all your tumbling for three or four months you should certainly be able to achieve perfection at the end of that time. Experiment with longer or shorter runs, different amounts of grit and polish, and pebbles of different hardnesses. This is the best way to serve your apprenticeship in tumbling and it will soon make you a master or mistress of the art. Nothing should go very wrong if you follow each step, each process, logically. If it does, reference to past experience should soon put matters right. On page oo, for quick guidance, is a list of common faults and suggested causes.

Fault finding

Fault	Possible cause
Machine runs intermittently, or stops	Badly wired plug; lubrication of bearings not carried out; oil on drive belt or rollers
Pebbles still rough after first and second grind	Overloaded barrel; insufficient grit; barrel slipping on rollers; hard and soft pebbles mixed
Pebbles badly cracked after first grind	Underloaded barrel; poor specimens
Inferior polish achieved	Second stage grind not long enough; insufficient polish; hard and soft pebbles mixed in barrel
Flats develop on pebbles	Underloaded barrel; speed of revolution too slow
Leaking barrel	Caps not fitted correctly; grit particles not removed from cap and/or barrel

5 Jewellery making

Let me make one point absolutely clear at the very outset: jewellery made with tumble-polished pebbles is not imitation jewellery. Each piece you make—ring, pendant, brooch or bracelet—is exclusively yours. No two pebbles are exactly alike and nobody else will ever make or own jewellery exactly the same. Select your pebbles carefully, choose your fittings wisely, make the piece to the best of your ability and the end product will be an object of beauty and originality which will give pleasure forever.

Baroque jewellery, as all jewellery made from tumble-polished pebbles is known, is extremely simple to create. Essentially it involves nothing more than gluing pebbles to fittings and perhaps bending a few pieces of wire; yet at the same time it allows you to use you artistic flair to decide the colour, size, shape, balance and final appearance of every piece you make. All of the art which goes into the making of costly pieces in diamond, emerald or pearl can be found in the best pieces of baroque jewellery and the fact that you found your 'gems' on a beach should in no way lower your artistic aims.

Basic equipment

You have just spent several weeks producing perfectly polished pebbles so a little time spent getting together the other basic materials of the craft should not be begrudged. There are not many, so let us go through them carefully:

A pair of short, thin-nosed pliers are all you should ever

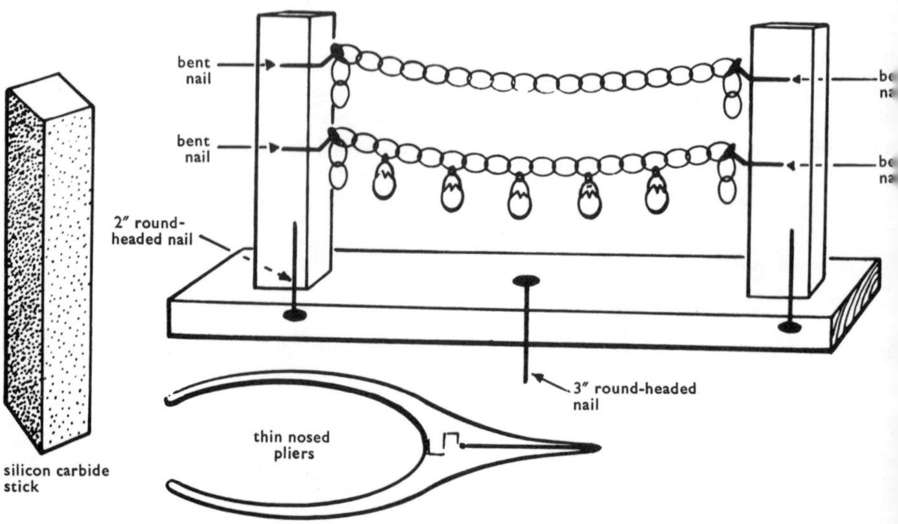

Fig. 26 Essential equipment

bent nail

bent nail

be na

be na

2″ round-headed nail

3″ round-headed nail

thin nosed pliers

silicon carbide stick

need for bending or straightening wire and they are a worthwhile buy for two reasons. They will save time and will do a neater job than fingers alone could ever do. Luckier readers might find an old pair in a tool box or garage, but if you have to buy, they should cost no more than 50p.

A silicon carbide abrasive stick is nothing more than a solid piece of the very abrasive you have used already to grind your pebbles to smoothness. In stick form it is ideal for roughening up fittings and stones prior to gluing. It costs very little.

A wooden jig will provide you with a very useful second pair of hands to hold chains and bracelets when attaching mounted stones. It can be made by anyone capable of using a hammer and nails. Buy three pieces of 2 in. × 1 in. softwood, all nine inches long. Hammer two one-and-a-half inch, narrow-headed nails about halfway into the narrower side of one of your pieces of wood. The first nail should be fixed two inches from the end of the block; the second near the middle. Next, do exactly the same to your second piece of wood. Now nail your third piece across the top of the two pieces you have hammered nails into, making sure that the protruding nails point inwards towards each other. Now turn the whole thing upside down, bend the protruding nails upwards to an angle by tapping them with your hammer, and your jig is made. If you are lucky enough to have a workbench you can nail the jig to the bench for extra support.

Item four on your list should be very easy to get hold of. This is an *old grill pan* or *shallow roasting tin*. The lid of a biscuit tin would serve almost as well, though it is rather shallow and the grill pan's handle will be found most useful. The container is filled with sand and its purpose is to hold pebbles while fittings are being glued to them. The pebbles are pressed firmly into the sand, thus leaving both hands free for placing the glued fittings in position. As the adhesive used takes some time to set, the sand tray ensures a safe place for the pebbles during the hardening period and leaves you free to continue with other tasks.

Fig. 27 The grill pan makes an ideal container for the sand and pebbles

A small piece of glass or *plastic-laminated board* is useful as a mixing palette when preparing the adhesive. Both can be easily cleaned after use and, their surfaces being non-absorbent, there is no danger of contaminating the adhesive.

The adhesive is an epoxy resin (e.g. Araldite). It is an all-purpose adhesive and you are quite likely to have some already either in the garage or your tool box. If not, a box should cost less than 40p. and for this you will obtain sufficient to make many hundreds of jewellery items. The box contains two tubes—one the resin, the other the hardener. Before use, correct quantities from each tube must be thoroughly mixed together on a clean, dry, non-absorbent surface (hence your piece of glass), and the resultant mixture must be used within a very short time. Unlike ordinary glue, epoxy resin sets and hardens by a chemical process which cannot be stopped once the hardener and resin have been mixed. For this reason only very small quantities, ideally the exact amount you need to make a particular batch of jewellery items, should be mixed at any one time.

For applying the epoxy resin to the fittings before gluing I have found different-sized *darning needles* to be ideal. Push the points into small corks and use the eyed ends to pick up the small quantities of adhesive used to glue each piece.

Fig. 28 More useful equipment

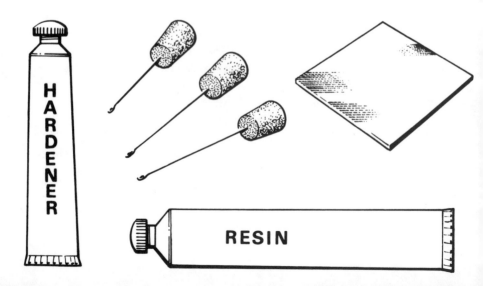

Finally, we come to the jewellery fittings themselves. **Fittings**
(*See* p. 78.) There are hundreds for you to chose from—
rings, bracelets, chains, earwires, earscrews, brooches,
cuff-links, tie bars, tie tacks, keyrings, necklaces—all in a
wide variety of styles and finishes. They can be purchased
in a selection of metals—sterling silver, gold, silver-plated,
gold-plated, stainless steel, or simply gold and silver
coloured alloy—and your choice depends on what you
wish to pay. But whatever metal or style of fitting you
select, there are only two basic ways in which your pebbles
are attached to the mountings. They are the *bell cap*
method or the *pad* method.

A *bell cap* is used to make pendants, necklaces, bracelets
and earrings. It consists, as its name suggests, of a hollow,
bell-shaped body surmounted by a tiny ring and it is secured,
cap-like, onto the pebble. The bell-shaped body is made
up of flexible, petal-like prongs of metal which are very
easy to bend.

They can be moulded with the fingers to fit snugly over
the end of any pebble where they are secured with epoxy
resin. The bell-capped pebble can then be fixed to a chain,
bracelet, or earwire by means of a *jump ring*. This is a
small circle of springy metal which can be opened, using
a pair of thin-nosed pliers, to allow the ring at the top of
the bell cap and a link from a piece of chain or a bracelet
to be coupled together.

Fig. 29 Bell caps (*top*) and jump rings
(*bottom*)

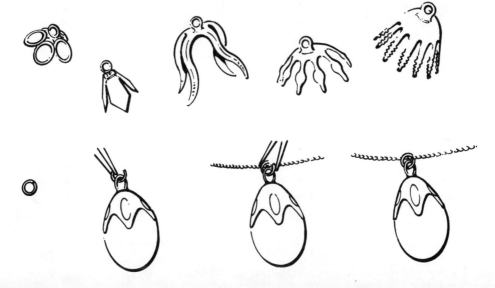

Fig. 30 'Pad' type fittings, useful for
rings, brooches and cufflinks

Both bell caps and jump rings come in several sizes. The smallest bell caps are no longer than match heads while the largest can be half an inch long. Jump rings to suit each size available and the size required depends on the size of the pebble, the aim always being to use the smallest possible bell cap and jump ring whatever the piece being made.

The *pad* method of fixing is used to make rings, brooches, cufflinks and other items in which the pebble is attached directly to the fitting and not hung onto it by means of a bell cap. Once again sizes differ, particularly in rings and bracelets, and the choice of fitting is determined by the size of pebble you wish to use for the job.

Making the jewellery

Let us now go step-by-step through the work involved in making some pieces of jewellery using both methods of fixing. First find yourself a clear working area in the kitchen and lay out your equipment as follows:

Pebbles. Select the very best of your round and pear-shaped pebbles for bell-capping and set aside any with a flat side for pad mounting.

Sand tray. Prepare this (salt can be used if sand is not readily available) by filling to a depth of two inches and shaking until level. Press your pebbles into the sand to about half their depth, making sure that the more pointed ends are upwards. Space them evenly across the tray.

Bell caps. Take various sizes, spread the prongs and sit one on top of each pebble. Experiment with different sizes and types to achieve the best possible artistic effect. Bear in mind that the position of the eye on the top of the

76

cap determines how the pebble will hang from the jump ring. If you want a particular side of a pebble to face 'forwards' you must position your bell cap accordingly.

Do not touch the tops of your pebbles with your fingers at this stage. Hold them around their middles. The oil in your skin can prevent a good bond when you cement the bell caps in position.

Epoxy resin. Do not start to mix this until you are quite satisfied that all bell caps selected are suitable. Then, having read the instructions carefully, squeeze the correct amount of resin and hardener on to your glass plate and mix very thoroughly.

Needles. Take a corked needle and pick up a small amount of mixed adhesive on the 'eye' end. Lift up your first bell cap and carefully place a blob of adhesive inside the cap. Replace the cap on the pebble and press down firmly. At this stage the adhesive is *not* holding the cap in position. The cap is balanced on top of the pebble and it is important that it remains balanced for the next hour so do not set it at an odd angle on the pebble.

Continue to lift and replace each pebble with its blob of adhesive until you have worked your way through the tray.

Leaving your tray on the workbench, light the grill of your cooker and turn it as high as possible. Let it burn for a few minutes, then carefully carry your tray of bell-capped pebbles from the bench and place it under the burning grill. Watch the prongs of the bell caps very carefully at this stage. After thirty seconds or so you will see the adhesive begin to flow from underneath the bell cap. The moment this happens pull out the tray. This must be done quickly, but gently. If the tray is knocked, all the bell caps will fall off.

Place the tray on a level surface away from heat and do not touch it for the next hour. When one hour has passed every bell cap will be firmly cemented to its pebble and the adhesive will have dried clear, colourless and almost unnoticeable.

If working with children or in a spot where access to a

Plate 6 Jewellery fittings

Plate 7 Jewellery to be proud of

hot grill is impossible, the tray of pebbles can be left to bond without heat quite successfully. Proceed as above until every bell cap has been replaced with its blob of adhesive on its pebble and leave the tray undisturbed for twenty-four hours. An equally good bond should be the result.

To return for a moment to the faster 'grill' method it is most important that the adhesive is not 'overcooked'. Remove the tray from under the grill the moment you see the epoxy begin to run. If this is not done it will discolour on hardening to an unpleasant brown.

The jig. When gluing is completed you can proceed to make necklaces, pendants and bracelets. Hook pieces of chain or bracelet onto the bent nails of your jig; work out the correct spacing of each pebble; and slip jump rings through the links on the chain or bracelet where required with the aid of your pliers. Select bell-capped pebbles according to shape, size and colour, and, using your pliers once again, couple them to your chain or bracelet by means of the jump rings.

Although slightly different methods are used for pad fittings, the aim remains the same: a perfect bond between fitting and pebble. This is best achieved by roughening the two surfaces to be joined with your *silicon carbide stick*. A few scratches on the pad and two or three strokes of the stick across the pebbles are all that is required.

Rings should be scratched in this way and then set in the sand tray in the same way as the pebbles were set for bell-capping. Scratch the area of the pebbles you wish to join to the ring pad *before* you mix your adhesive and proceed as for bell-capping. If using the quicker 'grill' method for bonding it will be found that the epoxy takes a few seconds longer to flow because it is protected from the heat by the pebble. How much longer depends on the size of the pebble because a larger pebble shields the resin from the heat far more than does a small pebble. It is probably better, therefore, to make rings with similar-sized stones in one batch.

Cufflinks and earscrews should be dealt with in the same

80

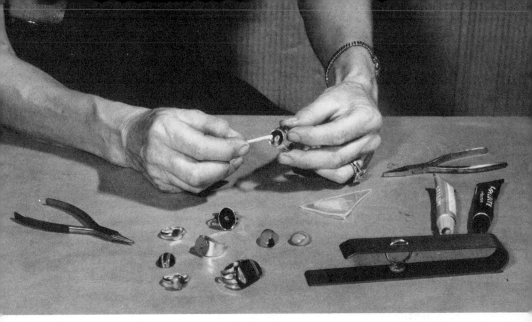

way as rings. Set the fitting in the sand tray after scratching the pad with the abrasive stick and glue the pebble to the fitting.

Bracelets should be laid out on the sand after each pad has been scratched. Pebbles of different sizes, shapes, and colours can then be tried on the pads before they are scratched and cemented. Again, it is probably better to work with pebbles of similar sizes.

Figs. 31 (a) and (b) Another method of ensuring a perfect bond between pebble and fitting without using heat. The spring steel clip on the right of the pictures holds the fitting and pebble securely in position until the adhesive has hardened.

Plate 8 Rough Foreign stones

Snowflake obsidian   Sodalite   Amethyst   Rutilated quartz
    Red tiger's eye   Rose quartz   Blue lace agate
      Aventurine   Rhodonite   Amazonite

Plate 9 The polished versions

Snowflake obsidian   Sodalite   Amethyst   Rutilated quartz
    Red tiger's eye   Rose quartz   Blue lace agate
        Aventurine   Rhodonite   Amazonite

There are so many different types of *brooches* available that the choice of whether to place the fitting or the pebble in the sand tray must be left to you. If you can balance the brooch on top of the pebble without fear of it slipping or falling off before the adhesive has dried, I would recommend that method. But if you feel safer with the fitting in the sand, allow a few seconds longer under the grill.

Finally, remember that the standard of jewellery you make rests entirely with you. If you use poor quality fittings, chipped or poorly polished pebbles, and far too much adhesive, the end product will be Junk! If you follow carefully the instructions set out above and use only your very best pebbles for jewellery-making the end product will give you great pleasure for many years.

Fig. 32 Attaching a polished pebble to a bell cap fitting to make a pendant. Again the spring steel clip will hold both in position until the adhesive has hardened

Once you have achieved success at polishing British pebbles you might like to turn your attention to pebbles and stones from other lands. These are within everyone's reach whether or not you take holidays abroad. Lapidary shops are opening in all parts of the country and if you visit one you will be able to buy rough broken fragments of a suitable size for tumbling from many parts of the world. I have not yet come upon a shop selling foreign pebbles, but this does not present a great problem for the tumble-polishing enthusiast. Rock fragments can be used to load a tumbler barrel if the first stage coarse grind is lengthened to allow the silicon carbide to remove rough edges and transform the rough rock to pebble shape.

If you are able to take a holiday on a foreign coast you will find all the exotic pebbles you can carry home in a rainbow range of colours that will delight your eye, captivate your imagination—and grossly overload your luggage for the journey home! I will repeat my earlier warning about not overloading yourself, though I realize the temptation will be great if your collecting in Britain has been confined to a few miles of coastline. You must, of course, still be ruthless in rejecting cracked or badly pitted specimens. However attractive, they will not polish well. Again, the rules about size and shape apply equally on a foreign beach. You will be making jewellery with the pebbles you select once you get them home and this must be kept in mind when collecting.

The pebbles you collect can be sorted into 'hard' and 'soft' groups, using the steel file and penknife blade, and you will be able to polish all pebbles in your 'hard' bag together without difficulty. Best results will be achieved with softer pebbles if they are polished separately because variations in the hardness of 'soft' material can be very wide; whereas most of the 'hard' material is likely to belong to the quartz family. Bear in mind that you will often come across familiar pebbles however far you go. Jaspers and agates and other easily recognizable varieties are to be found all over the world—though in deeper or more striking shades and colours. They can be treated in the

6 Exotic stones from foreign lands

Grouping

same way as those found in Britain.

I must emphasize the importance of keeping careful records when polishing unfamiliar foreign pebbles. Retain unpolished specimens of each type for later comparisons and, if stocks are plentiful, experiment with different grinding and polishing times.

Incidentally, I know of one enterprising young lady who has never spent a holiday south of Dover and yet she has foreign pebbles galore in her unpolished stocks. She hit on the bright idea of acquiring penfriends who live near the coast in half a dozen foreign countries and they keep her well stocked with pebbles in exchange for 'British-home-made' jewellery at Christmas and birthday times. It is an idea well worth copying if it is not possible to travel.

Lapidary shops

Readers who are able to visit lapidary shops or buy rough rock fragments by mail order will be delighted at the varieties obtainable in Britain. The first thing to do is write for lists and catalogues, which are available from most suppliers, and compare stocks and prices. A number of suppliers sell only in large quantities which would be uneconomical if you are using one tumbler with a single

Fig. 33 Inside a lapidary shop an assistant helps a customer choose the right polished stone for a ring fitting. Such shops have a huge selection of stones on show and welcome browsers

barrel; but the price saving, particularly on postage, makes bulk buying an attractive proposition for clubs and groups. However, I do not recommend the purchase of unbroken rock which, although much cheaper, is very difficult to reduce to tumble-polishing size unless you have a crushing machine. It is most unwise to attempt to break large pieces of rock with cold chisels and hammers, but if you are tempted, protect your eyes by wearing goggles.

Ready broken rock for tumble-polishing comes in a number of grades and I recommend the purchase of First Grade material wherever possible. This will be a little more expensive but badly cracked and poor quality material will have been rejected before weighing. If you buy Second Grade material you will have to do the rejecting yourself and this could reduce by as much as one-third the amount of suitable material you get for your money.

Terms such as 'First Grade' and 'Top Quality' are relative and their meaning depends on the overall quality of the material the supplier handles. In time you will acquire the knowledge to judge quality for yourself, but in the meanwhile you should buy from a supplier who sells under a 'Money back if not satisfied' guarantèe. All reputable suppliers sell under those terms.

Vast quantities of semi-precious rock are imported into Britain each year for use in the jewellery and lapidary trades. Many of the varieties are far too costly to be considered suitable for polishing in a tumbler. They are used by jewellers who cut and facet them and often set them alongside precious gems in rings, bracelets and pendants which sell for many hundreds of pounds. Nevertheless a wide choice remains open to the amateur tumble-polisher who requires something beautiful at only pence per pound. Some of those stones you should look out for are listed below. When polishing these materials aim for the same perfection you should now have reached with British beach pebbles and do not be afraid to experiment with longer or shorter grinding and polishing stages. Trial and error backed by detailed notes and records will soon lead you to perfection with these unfamiliar foreigners.

Summary of foreign stones

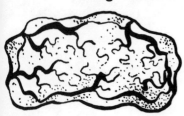

Fig. 34 Section through a moss agate

Fig. 35 A scenic agate

Fig. 36 Malachite

Name	*Description*
Moss agate	Translucent with mossy, fernlike 'growths' which are best seen when the rock is held up to light. Usually green.
Blue lace agate	Opaque and very finely banded. A delicate light blue in colour; the 'lace' effect best seen in rough rock
Scenic agate	Opaque to transluscent with internal forms which suggest forest and mountain scenery
Plume agate	Transluscent. Internal formations suggest smoke and feathers
Banded agate	Opaque to transluscent. Distinctive banding in a wide colour range including white, blue, yellow, green, brown, red, and black
Malachite	Opaque. Rich deep green in colour with feint banding best seen when polished
Sodalite	Transluscent. Deep blue, often with white streaks
Snowflake obsidan	Opaque. Black with snowflake patterns
Tiger eye	Opaque. Silky yellow and brown with a 'catseye' effect when turned in light. Red and blue varieties are also available

88

Tumbling hints
Agate has a hardness of 7 on Moh's Scale and all rough agate is difficult to grind smooth. It does, however, take a wonderful polish if the first grinding stage is not cut short. Tumble three or four times as long as you would first-grind beach agates. If your first attempts at polishing agate are unsuccessful try putting the stones through two long coarse stages and change the grit after the first run. Some agates are often badly cracked when purchased in tumbling sizes and it is best to tumble two loads on the first grind and select the best for second stage grinding and polishing. All rough agates can be tumbled together

As above

As above

As above

As above

A very soft stone (Hardness 4) which should be tumbled separately. Inspect every twelve hours when first-stage grinding and do not overrun. A fairly expensive stone which might tempt you to underload the barrel. Beautiful when polished well

Softer than agate but harder than malachite (Hardness 5). Probably best tumbled separately but should be successful with snowflake obsidian and rhodonite

Hardness 5—although variations in hardness occur in varieties from different parts of the world. Do not overrun on the second stage

This stone (Hardness 7) should always polish well, but much inferior material is on the market. Buy only First Grade and do not underrun the first stage. Will tumble with other quartz material

Name	Description
Amethyst	Transparent and semi-transparent. Pale to deep purple, often with white markings
Lapis lazuli	Opaque. Blue and white speckled with gold-coloured pyrites
Rose quartz	Transluscent. Pale pink
Jasper	Opaque. Red and brown with coloured patterns
Rhodonite	Opaque. Red and pink with black markings
Rhodochrosite	Opaque. Red and pink bands streaked with white
Cornelian	Semi-transparant. Orange to deep red
Aventurine	Transluscent. Green with a sparkle throughout
Bloodstone	Opaque. Deep green with tiny red spots
Rutilated quartz	Transparent. Clear quartz with golden needles running through
Amazonite	Opaque to transluscent. Deep green to blue with a sparkle

Note: Many suppliers offer mixed bags of rock of similar hardness for tumbling. They make excellent buys if First Quality material only is included.

Another quartz (Hardness 7) which should polish well. Again, there is a great deal of poor quality material on the market. The best quality is usually only available in very small fragments and if you are lucky enough to locate a good supply you should tumble it separately and watch for cracks on the first and second grinding stages

A difficult stone to tumble-polish really well (Hardness 5). Tumble separately and do not overrun the first stage or underrun the second stage

A beautiful stone when polished well (Hardness 7). Should tumble with other quartz. Watch out for cracks during the first grind

An inexpensive stone which can look beautiful when polished (Hardness 6–7). Variations in hardness might present difficulties but should polish with other quartz. If unsuccessful tumble separately with a longer first stage

(Hardness 5–6). Difficult to find good quality material. Tumble separately for best results

Very soft (Hardness 3). Tumble separately with a very short first stage

Polishes perfectly when first stage is not underrun (Hardness 7). Tumble with other quartz

A long first stage should give excellent results (Hardness 7). Tumble with other quartz

Beautiful when polished (Hardness 7). Tumble with other quartz

Tumble with other quartz (Hardness 7)

Tumble separately for best results (Hardness 6)

7 More advanced machines

I said at the beginning of this book that lapidary grows on you. It is a fascinating subject and if you have enjoyed tumble-polishing beach pebbles you can look forward to many years of pleasure should you decide to pursue the hobby at a more advanced level. Machines to help you progress and develop your skills at the craft are not terribly expensive and the jewellery you will be able to make once you have learned the more advanced techniques will quickly repay your initial outlay on equipment, either in sheer pleasure or in a good profit should you wish to sell your products. Whether you choose to teach yourself at home or join one of the many evening classes or lapidary clubs which are now run in most towns, your complete enjoyment is guaranteed.

One of the first tasks beginners like to attempt is slicing a beach pebble to produce two perfectly matched half pebbles to make into cuff-links or earrings. As you have already discovered, pebbles can be extremely hard and the only suitable tool for slicing them is a *diamond saw*. This is a circular metal disc, eight to ten inches in diameter, and

Fig. 37 Slicing a piece of rock on a diamond saw. Pebbles can also be sliced in half to make a pair of earrings or cufflinks

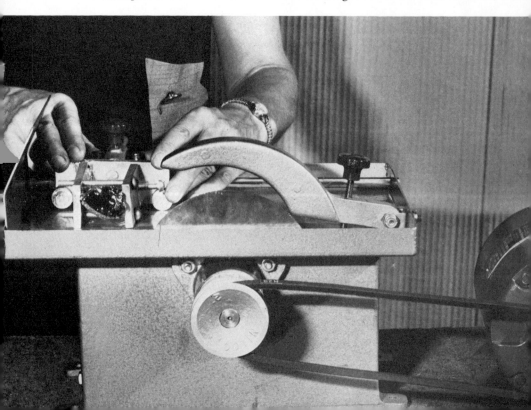

approximately one-tenth of an inch thick. The disc has
diamond particles embedded into notches on its rim and
when it is made to turn on a shaft connected to an electric
motor, it will bite its way through the toughest semi-
precious pebble in a few seconds.

The diamond saw used to slice pebbles is known as a
trim saw and it is also used to cut pieces of rock to any
size required. The stone is usually held in a clamp which
the operator guides against the rim of the saw.

Please note that although the word 'saw' conjures up
images of dangerous sharp teeth, you need have no such
fears with a diamond saw. It has no teeth and will not cut
fingers—even when they are pressed against the rim. It
actually grinds it way through rock and is completely
safe to use even when working with children.

Another method of removing unwanted material from
a piece of stone or a pebble is by grinding. For this purpose
grinding wheels are used. They are made from the same
silicon carbide you use when tumble-polishing and they
are similarly obtainable in coarse, medium and fine grades.
The grinding wheel is also driven on a shaft connected to
an electric motor—often the same shaft as the one that
turns the diamond saw—and the stone or pebble to be
shaped is held against the wheel as it turns. On such wheels

Fig. 38 A selection of sawing, grinding
and polishing attachments

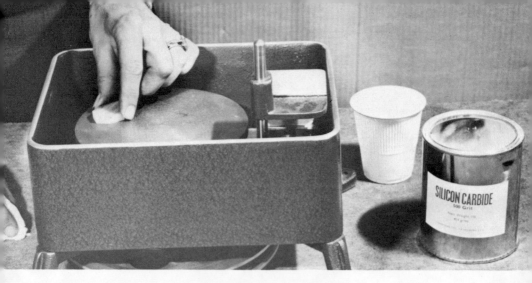

stones can be ground flat, or rough edges removed from fragments prior to polishing.

Polishing discs are also turned on a shaft driven by an electric motor. They are made from thick felt which can be impregnated with polishing powder. The stone to be polished is then pressed firmly against the wheel as it spins.

The cutting, grinding, and polishing of pebbles and stones is generally carried out on one machine. It is usual to purchase this 'bare' and add the various attachments as one progresses with the hobby. The great advantage of this idea is that the cost of equipment can be spread over a period of time.

Cast iron laps are used for grinding and polishing flat surfaces, particularly thin slabs of rock previously sliced on a diamond saw. The laps are mounted horizontally on a shaft in the same way as a gramophone record is placed on a turntable. Loose silicon carbide is then sprinkled onto the surface of the disc and the flat slab is pressed against the lap in order to grind it to the required finish. Grits are changed progressively and final polishing is carried out on a horizontal felt wheel.

Cabochon cutting is also carried out on silicon carbide wheels and felt discs. A cabochon is a stone or pebble which has been shaped to a symmetrical oval dome by first mounting the stone on a piece of stick (known as a

94

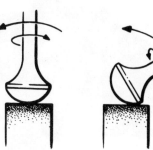

Figs. 40 and 41 The techniques of cabochon cutting. It is important to get a smooth, round surface on the dopped pebbles

dop stick) with hot wax and then grinding it to shape by moving it against a revolving wheel.

Faceting involves cutting flat faces on a stone in such a way that the beauty of the stone is revealed when light is refracted through it. Faceting attachments, which ensure the correct angle of cut on each face, can be purchased and attached to many machines; or one can buy a complete machine just for faceting.

Fig. 42 (a) Faceting a stone and (b) faceting attachments

Illustrated here are some of the many versatile lapidary machines on the market today:

Fig. 43 The 'Gem Master', a very popular, versatile model

Fig. 44 The 'Cabochon Master'

Fig. 45 The 'Rock Master' for larger stones

I must not close this book without a very brief mention of four subjects which might be of importance should you decide to make jewellery on a commercial scale. They are unlikely to effect readers interested only in making jewellery for personal use, but for the commercially minded the four subjects are: purchase tax; income tax; import duty; and the law relating to the removal of pebbles and rock samples from public beaches and mine and quarry workings.

At the time of writing, sales of jewellery are subject to purchase tax. If you plan to sell large quantities of home-made jewellery you should seek advice on the up-to-date position regarding purchase tax from your local office where expert guidance is available free of charge. Note that polished pebbles and stones themselves are not subject to purchase tax; it is only when fittings are attached to the stones that they are regarded as jewellery by the tax authorities.

All income is unfortunately subject to income tax and you should always keep careful records of any transactions —both buying and selling—if you aim to earn any income from the hobby. The services of an accountant are recommended if your knowledge of book-keeping is limited and you aim to make substantial sales.

Import duty is not payable at the time of writing on rough rock, pebbles, and minerals purchased from abroad. You should not run into difficulties when passing through Customs points after collecting pebbles or rock fragments while on holiday.

The removal of large quantities of shingle from public beaches is carefully controlled by local authorities. Shingle acts as a natural barrier against erosion and its uncontrolled removal could result in large areas of land and foreshore being eaten away by the sea. A few pounds of pebbles taken home by a tumble-polishing enthusiast will not make the slightest difference, but all collecting should be kept to a minimum.

If you wish to collect rock samples inland, bear in mind that all land, including old mines and quarries, is owned by

8 Rules and regulations

someone and you will certainly lay yourself open to a charge of trespassing if you climb fences or ignore 'keep out' notice boards. It is rarely difficult to obtain permission to collect a few samples if the correct approach is used. Be polite, explain your hobby, ask first and say 'thank you' afterwards and you should have few problems wherever you go.

Lapidary suppliers This is by no means a comprehensive list of lapidary suppliers, but merely a guide to some of the larger establishments operating throughout the country.

Tumble-polishing machines and rough stones:

Gemrocks Ltd, 20/30 Holborn, London E.C.1.

Webb-Fletcher (Tumblers) Ltd, Suites 11/12, 52 Shaftesbury Avenue, London, W.1.

M. L. Beach (Products) Ltd, Church Street, Twickenham, Middlesex.

P.M.R. Lapidary Supplies, Smithy House, Atholl Road, Pitlochry, Perth.

Kernowcraft Ltd, 68 Highertown, Truro, Cornwall.

Gemstones, 35 Princes Avenue, Hull, Yorks.

Jewellery fittings:

Doreen Jewellery Mounts, Suites 11/12, 52 Shaftesbury Avenue, London, W.1.

Maps, semi-precious stone locations:

Treasure Hunters' Research and Information Bureau, Suites 11/12, 52 Shaftesbury Avenue, London, W.1.

Maps showing the locations of pebbles

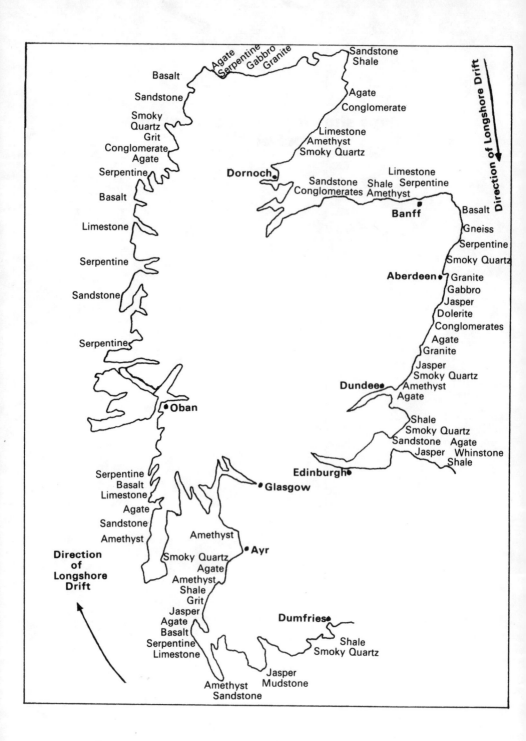

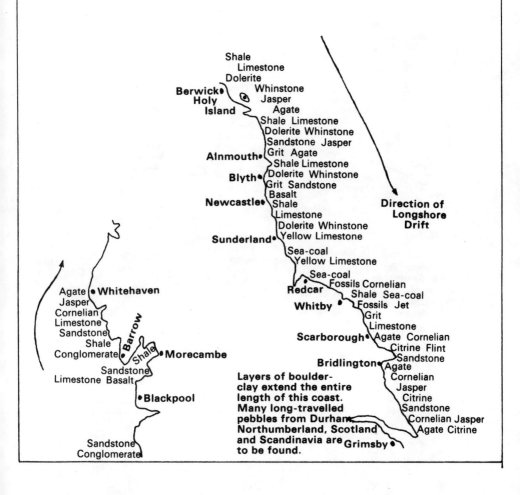

Shale
Limestone
Dolerite
Berwick• Whinstone
Holy Jasper
Island Agate
Shale Limestone
Dolerite Whinstone
Sandstone Jasper
Grit Agate
Ainmouth• Shale Limestone
Blyth• Dolerite Whinstone
Grit Sandstone
Basalt
Newcastle• Shale
Limestone
Dolerite Whinstone
Sunderland• Yellow Limestone
Sea-coal
Yellow Limestone
Sea-coal
Redcar• Fossils Cornelian
Shale Sea-coal
Whitby Fossils Jet
Grit
Limestone
Scarborough• Agate Cornelian
Citrine Flint
Sandstone
Bridlington• Agate
Cornelian
Jasper
Citrine
Sandstone
Cornelian Jasper
Agate Citrine

**Direction of
Longshore
Drift**

Agate • **Whitehaven**
Jasper
Cornelian
Limestone
Sandstone
Shale
Conglomerate **Barrow**
Shale • **Morecambe**
Sandstone
Limestone Basalt

• **Blackpool**

Sandstone
Conglomerate

Layers of boulder-
clay extend the entire
length of this coast.
Many long-travelled
pebbles from Durham,
Northumberland, Scotland
and Scandinavia are
to be found. **Grimsby** •

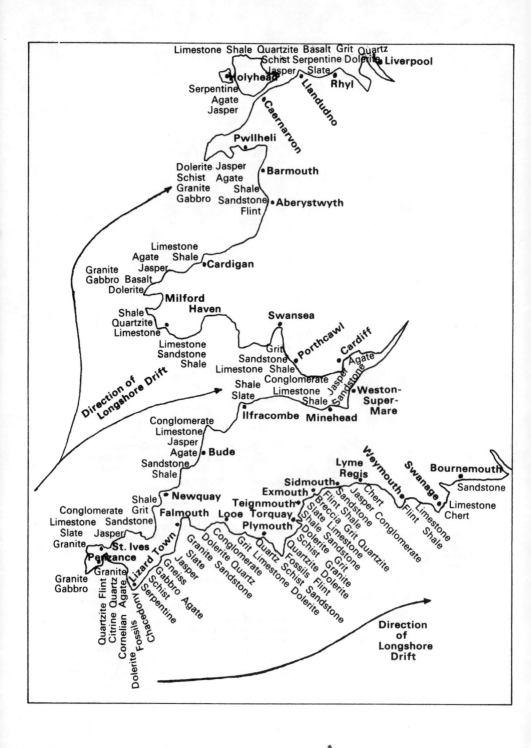

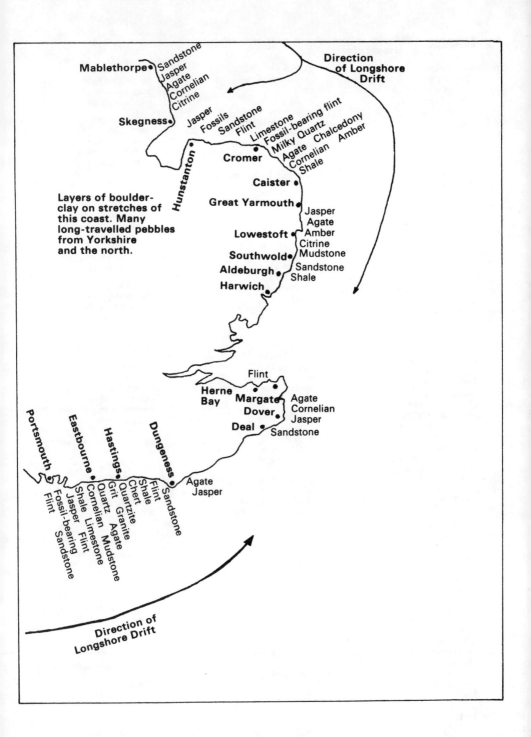

Mablethorpe • Sandstone
Jasper
Agate
Cornelian
Citrine

Direction
of Longshore
Drift

Skegness • Jasper
Fossils
Sandstone
Flint
Limestone
Fossil-bearing flint
Milky Quartz
Agate Chalcedony Amber
Cornelian
Shale

Hunstanton •

Cromer •

Caister •

Great Yarmouth •

Layers of boulder-
clay on stretches of
this coast. Many
long-travelled pebbles
from Yorkshire
and the north.

Lowestoft • Jasper
Agate
Amber
Citrine
Southwold • Mudstone
Aldeburgh • Sandstone
Harwich • Shale

Flint

Herne
Bay
Margate • Agate
Dover • Cornelian
Jasper
Deal • Sandstone

Portsmouth
Eastbourne •
Hastings •
Dungeness •
Sandstone
Agate
Jasper

Flint
Shale
Quartzite
Quartz Granite
Cornelian Agate
Shale Flint Limestone
Jasper Mudstone
Fossil-bearing
Flint
Sandstone

Chert
Grit

Direction of
Longshore Drift

Index
The figures in bold refer to pages on which colour illustrations occur.